DARE TO WALK ON WATER

52 Dares to be

TREASURING GOD

Robert A. Allen

Cover illustration by David Allen

Printed in the United States of America

First printing, 2018

ISBN-9781980740513

The Bible Story Family

P.O. Box 28342

Minneapolis, MN 55428-3551

www.thebiblestoryfamily.com

What people are saying about this book.

"Normally one dares another to do something reckless. However, in this book Dr. Robert Allen dares his readers to do something purposeful. That is, the author dares us to pursue God with purposeful steps of faith. The reward is knowing God like never before. Accept the challenge. Take the Dare. Treasure God."

> Dr. Matt Morrell
> Senior Pastor, Fourth Baptist Church
> President, Central Baptist Theological
> Seminary

"The main purpose of this book is to encourage believers to have an awe-inspiring view of God that will change the way they live. A worthy goal and one that should be the desire of every Christian. The author does this in a simple, engaging, and profound manner. If one wishes to follow all the suggestions in the 52 chapters, the goal will, I believe, be accomplished."

> Gordon Taylor
> Coordinator at Reformed Baptist Network

To

Arthur Allen, Don Odens, Earl Miller,

Jerry Falwell and Alan Potter

who taught and modeled action-oriented Bible
communication

to my eternal benefit.

DARE TO WALK ON WATER

TREASURING GOD

52 PRACTICAL WAYS TO KNOW GOD BETTER

TABLE OF CONTENTS

Dare Seven: A Beautiful God – Psalm 27:4

Dare Eight: An Eternal God – Deuteronomy 33:27

Dare Nine: An Infinite God – I Kings 8:27

Dare Ten: God Who Never Changes – James 1:17

Dare Eleven: God Immaterial – Colossians 1:15

Dare Twelve: God is Life – Jeremiah 10:10

Dare Thirteen: A God Who Knows All –

     Romans 11:33

Dare Fourteen: God All-Wise – Romans 16:27

Dare Fifteen: God our Refuge – Psalm 46:1

Dare Sixteen: God our Joy – Nehemiah 8:10

Dare Seventeen: God our Song – Exodus 15:2

Dare Eighteen: God Transcendent – Ezekiel 1:28

Dare Nineteen: God is Light – John 1:4-5

Dare Twenty: God Omnipresent – Psalm 139:8-10

Dare Twenty-One: God is Faithful – II Timothy 2:13

Dare Twenty-Two: God is Good – Psalm 33:5

Dare Twenty-Three: God is Just – Psalm 97:1-2

Dare Twenty-Four: God is Mercy – Psalm 136:1

Dare Twenty-Five: God is Love - I John 4:8

Dare Twenty-Six: God is Holy – Isaiah 6:3

Dare Twenty-Seven: God is Sovereign –

     I Timothy 6:15

Dare Twenty-Eight: God is Truth – John 14:6

Dare Twenty-Nine: God Almighty – Revelation 19:6

Dare Thirty: God is Grace – Ephesians 1:7

Dare Thirty-One: God is Awake – Psalm 121:4

Dare Thirty-Two: God is Gentle – Galatians 5:23

Dare Thirty-Three: God is Longsuffering –

     Galatians 5:22

Dare Thirty-Four: God is Peace – Galatians 5:22

Dare Thirty-Five: God is Self-Controlled –

     Galatians 5:22-23

Dare Thirty-Six: God is Meek – Galatians 5:22-23

Dare Thirty-Seven: God is Like Water –

     Jeremiah 17:13

Dare Thirty-Eight: God is Like Rock –

     II Samuel 22:2-3

Dare Thirty-Nine: God as Father – Matthew 6:9

Dare Forty: God the Alpha and Omega –

     Revelation 1:8

Dare Forty-One: God Who is Enough – Genesis 17:1

Dare Forty-Two: God Cares – I Peter 5:7

All Scripture quotations are from the New International Version unless otherwise noted.

THE DARE

"I dare you! I double-dog dare you!"

Remember those childhood challenges? Almost impossible to refuse, although I never have figured out exactly what a double dog might look like.

You have been saved for several years now. You attend church regularly. You read your Bible along with devotional books designed to increase your understanding of Scripture. In many ways you have matured as a believer and grown in faith. You trust God. You pray.

You know God! Really? You know about George Washington and Abraham Lincoln and Teddy Roosevelt, but do you know them? History teaches us facts about people just as the Bible teaches us facts about God. But one of the amazing truths of life in Christ involves knowing God beyond the simple accumulation of facts. We need to know the facts, but we also need to go beyond that and enter into a relationship with God.

What does it mean to "love the Lord your God with all your heart and with all your soul and with all your mind and with all your strength." (Mark 12:30). Is it possible to love the Lord with all our thoughts, but not with all our emotions and will and actions? Is it possible to know truth about God without a transformation of our hearts, a decision to obey and a corresponding change in what we do? Loving God with heart, soul, mind and strength requires valuing God above every other possession. Do we really treasure God?

Enter the DARE!

DARE to walk on water.

"Immediately Jesus made the disciples get into the boat and go on ahead of him to the other side, while he dismissed the crowd. After he had dismissed them, he went up on a mountainside by himself to pray. Later that night, he was there alone, and the boat was already a considerable distance from land, buffeted by the waves because the wind was against it. Shortly before dawn Jesus went out to them, walking on the lake. When the disciples saw him walking on the lake, they were terrified. "It's a ghost," they said, and cried out in fear. But Jesus immediately said to them: "Take courage! It is I. Don't be afraid." "Lord, if it's you," Peter replied, "tell me to come to you on the water." "Come," he said. Then Peter got down out of the boat, walked on the water and came toward Jesus. But when he saw the wind, he was afraid and, beginning to sink, cried out, "Lord, save me!" Immediately Jesus reached out his hand and caught him. "You of little faith," he said, "why did you doubt?" And when they climbed into the boat, the wind died down. Then those who were in the boat worshiped him, saying, "Truly you are the Son of God." Matthew 14:22-33

Do the impossible. Get out of the boat. Rock it if you need to. Tip the entire ship over if that is what it takes to get you into the water. Knowing God extends far beyond Sunday worship. No one really knows God until they have walked with Him on the water. Know how to spend time with Him when we need comfort. Know how He treats us when we sin. Know how God teaches us what He does in order to make us like Christ. Knowing God means applying mental facts about Him to every practical part of life in this world and in the world to come.

Take the challenge! Accept the dare!

Run to Christ on top of the waves. After all, no one can walk on the water without His help. So, run to Him and walk on the water in pursuit of truly knowing and treasuring God.

This book is one of a five-part series:

Dare to Walk on Water: Treasuring God

Dare to Walk on Water: Transformed by God

Dare to Walk on Water: Serving God

Dare to Walk on Water: Creative Like God

Dare to Walk on Water: The Workbook

Each book moves from an understanding and interpretation of scripture to practical application and action steps. They can be read in any order. *Dare to Walk on Water: The Workbook* enables in-depth Bible study, taking the reader into a life-long adventure of increased understanding and creative application of God's Word.

Dare One

Forget the God You Created

"These things you have done, and I have been silent;
you thought that I was one like yourself. But now I
rebuke you and lay the charge before you." (ESV)
Psalm 50:21

Science fiction writers have been describing aliens for many years. Fantastic images have been created through verbal and visual artistry. But for the most part those aliens have been very similar to humans. They may have green skin, but they have skin. They may have multiple arms but they still have arms. Their torsos may be topped with many heads, but those heads have eyes and ears and mouths. It is very difficult to create an alien who is totally other than what we know.

People have also been creating gods throughout history. Those gods almost always look like us. They may be stronger and taller and wiser, but they share certain attributes common to the human race.

Each one of us has created in our own minds an image of God. The psalmist tells us that we have come to think that He is like us. We have endowed Him with human attributes. It is true that we are like God in some ways, having been made in His image. But it is not true that He is like us. He is that totally Other being which our minds will never completely comprehend. There are manifold attributes of God which we will never discover with our rational minds. There are also attributes of God which we can know because He has revealed them to us.

Before we can learn the truth about God, we must cast aside our own images of Him which our minds have created. The rational method of knowing God will prevent us from a true understanding of His biblical revelation. Rational thinking tells us that God does not possess the imperfections found in humans (i.e.hatred). But notice where that argument can lead. Hatred of evil leads men into war against evil and war has become a terrible problem in modern society. So if God does not contain our imperfections, He must not share our hatred of evil. But we know from Scripture that God does hate evil and at times has even commanded that wars be fought to destroy evil. So rationally we have a dilemma in our human understanding of God.

Rational thinking says that God possesses to an infinite degree all perfections found in His creatures. So a person who believes that abortion is a better choice than bringing unwanted children into the word could conclude that God possesses what that person sees as a perfection and say that God favors abortion. But the Bible says just the opposite.

Rational thinking, arguing from something called causality, says that God must possess those attributes necessary to explain the world of nature and mind. So a person could argue that since sin and suffering exist in the world of nature God must be the cause of sin and suffering. Yet the Bible clearly teaches that God is not the author of sin. Discovery of God through rational thinking alone will cause a person to do exactly what the psalmist said would happen. He will create God just like himself.

DARE to see God as He reveals Himself in the Word of God. Destroy the image of God you have created in your own mind with all human limitations and failings. Allow yourself to discover a God who is totally Other. He is not like Moses. He is not like George Washington. He is not like Superman. He is not like Santa Claus. He is not like the Man Upstairs. He is not like anything else in the entire universe. Stretch your mind to infinite unlimitedness in order to catch a glimpse of a God uncontained by time, space or matter.

Set aside everything you have ever been told about God by this world and prepare to see Him in the phenomenal, transcendent glory in which He reveals Himself in the Word of God.

As you begin this adventure of treasuring God, fill a loose-leaf notebook with totally blank pages. As you read and interact with the Word of God, allow God Himself to reveal His works, attributes and essence to your mind. By the time you have completed 52 dares your notebook should be full of truth concerning this God you increasingly come to treasure.

Dare Two

God Without Limits

"Oh, the depth of the riches of the wisdom and
knowledge of God! How unsearchable his judgments,
and his paths beyond tracing out!"
Romans 11:33

Calvin Miller in *The Table of Inwardness*
writes, "One door opens to the world of the spirit:
imagination…to follow Christ we must create in our
minds God's unseen world, or never confront it at
all."
Aiden W. Tozer in *The Knowledge of the Holy* says,
"If we insist upon trying to imagine Him, we end with
an idol, made not with hands but with thoughts; and

an idol of the mind is as offensive to God as an idol of the hand." He goes on to add, "Whatever we visualize God to be—He is not."

On the one hand it is impossible as humans to think about God without engaging our imaginations. On the other hand, visualization easily morphs into a creation of God out of our own thoughts, desires and experiences. Finite thought will never succeed in understanding the infinite. As we come to understand God through those truths He has revealed about Himself, we can be satisfied with that understanding. At the same time, we must be careful not to indulge in speculation concerning those things He has not revealed. God will never be limited to what we can understand about Him. His total essence is incomprehensible to the human mind. We must be content with a God whom we cannot fully understand. We have a God without limits.

As you consider the truth about God which you will be discovering through the Scriptures, prepare your mind to envision every attribute without limits. One way to do that is to consider the unlimited nature of God in relation to the created universe. Although discoveries continue to be made, astronomers estimate that the farthest known galaxy from earth is about 13.1 billion light years away (Physics World, Oct. 23, 2013). God is not limited by that distance. He is just as present in that galaxy as He is in ours. In fact, God is not limited by space at all. He created space and lives not only within but beyond it. We must not limit our idea of God to the universe which He created. By the same token we must not limit our idea of God to the limits our mind envisions concerning wisdom or love, mercy or peace, faithfulness, truth, justice, holiness, goodness or any other attribute of God. All are unlimited.

Think about the words found in the hymn "The Love of God" by Frederick Lehman, based on lines written in 1050 by Meir Ben Isaac Nehorai.

"Could we with ink the ocean fill and were the sky of parchment made,

Were every stalk on earth a quill and every man a scribe by trade.

To write the love of God above would drain the ocean dry,

Nor could the scroll contain the whole though stretched from sky to sky."

DARE to apply that unlimited vision of God's attributes to everything you learn about Him from Scripture. What the Bible says is true and we can be satisfied with the knowledge it communicates to us about God. But we must never think that we know all there is to know about God, even if we master everything the Bible says about Him. As you take each of the following dares and record each attribute of God in your notebook, include the word "Infinite" beside it.

Infinite Love

Infinite Grace

Infinite Holiness

Infinite Power

Infinite Life

Infinite Wisdom

Infinite Joy

Referring to the index of this book, make a list of every attribute you will be studying and write each one down on a sheet of paper in your notebook along with the designation INFINITE.

DARE to remove all the limits your mind has placed on God in the past. Start all over again, accepting the truth He reveals concerning Himself.

Dare Three

God in Nature

"For since the creation of the world God's invisible
qualities—his eternal power and divine nature—have
been clearly seen, being understood from what has
been made, so that people are without excuse."
Romans 1:20

Several years ago, an individual living in
Arizona announced that she had seen the face of God
appearing in a tortilla. A shrine was constructed and
people made pilgrimages to see God in the tortilla.
Other claims to such sightings include a wooden door
on an Ikea furniture store, a baking tray in Yorkshire,
England, and in an airport flooring tile.

21

What does it mean to see God in nature? Should we be looking for images of God in tortillas and baking trays?

Paul clearly teaches that truth about God can be understood from His created world, specifically truth about his omnipotence and His divinity. We can look at the world in which we live and know that God is God and that He is powerful. Those are truths which are self-evident. Only One who is greater than the universe could have created the universe. Only One who possesses all power could have brought this world into existence. Those two facts alone are enough to remove any excuse for those who refuse to believe in God.

Careful observations of the physical world will also teach us other truths about God. We could circle the world seven times in one second if we could move at the speed of light. But it would still take four years at the same speed to arrive at Alpha Centauri, the nearest star to our sun. That nature fact should reveal to us the immensity and infinity of a Creator God.

The bolas spider captures its prey by swinging a single strand of web like a lasso and trapping insects for food. Reflecting on that one innovative arachnid technique we should realize that the God who created spiders possesses wisdom and creativity.

Throughout the temperate zones of the earth summer, fall, winter and spring continue in unbroken succession just as promised in Genesis 8:22,

"As long as the earth endures, seedtime and harvest,

cold and heat, summer and winter,

day and night will never cease."

We live in the midst of continual day and night, summer and winter, seedtime and harvest. It should teach us that God is faithful and unchanging.

The reason we do not look for the face of God in material objects is simply because God does not have a face. He sometimes describes Himself using human features so we can grasp the fact that He works—something which we associate with having hands, or that He sees—something we associate with having eyes. These are called anthropomorphisms. But God is Spirit, so no image people will ever see can be identified as an image of God.

Instead of looking for images of God in your breakfast cereal, train yourself to recognize evidences of Biblical truth concerning God in your observations of His creation. Think through the following list of natural science facts and write in your loose-leaf notebook as many truths about God as you can that come from the world in which we live.

DARE to see God in the natural world.

No two snowflakes are ever identical.

If you could take one teaspoon of material from a neutron star it would weigh six billion tons.

The lining of your stomach replaces itself every four days.

A jumping flea moves at 100 g with one g equal to the acceleration caused by gravity.

The Great Barrier Reef is the largest living structure on earth.

The known universe is composed of 50 billion galaxies with 100 billion to 1 trillion stars in each galaxy.

The human brain can take in 11 million bits of information every second.

There are 60,000 miles of blood vessels in the human body.

In your notebook, record one truth about God which increases His value to you as a result of each of those facts from nature. DARE to see God revealed in this wonderful, awesome universe which He created for us to inhabit, enjoy and observe in order to know Him.

Dare Four

God in Tri-Unity

"How much more, then, will the blood of Christ, who
through the eternal Spirit offered himself
unblemished to God, cleanse our consciences from
acts that lead to death,
so that we may serve the living God!"
Hebrews 9:14

Islam, Judaism and Christianity are often
referred to as monotheistic, meaning they all believe
in one God. At the same time Islamic scholars teach
that Christianity practices a form of polytheism or
belief in many Gods because of the doctrine of the
Trinity. "In the Muslim view, Christians also commit
this sin by believing in Jesus as the Son of God, for

God cannot have a son, that is, another being of the same nature as himself." (Burke, The Major Religions, Blackwell).

The Father, the Son and the Spirit are all called God in scripture. This passage in Hebrews is only one of several places where the three act together in perfect unity. The disciples were commanded to baptize "in the name of the Father and of the Son and of the Holy Spirit" (Matthew 28:19). All three persons of the Trinity were involved in creation, the atonement, the baptism of Christ, the work of salvation and the indwelling work of the Spirit.

Logically we cannot comprehend a Being who can be at once both Three and One. But the very fact that we cannot understand or explain the doctrine of the Trinity should actually increase our appreciation and evaluation of God. If we could understand everything about God, He would be no greater than our understanding. Remember, God is unlimited in every way.

DARE to base your understanding of God on an acceptance of His tri-unity. What is true of the Father is true of the Son and the Spirit. What is true of the Son and the Spirit is true of the Father. They are in complete unity and total agreement without any division even when they act in accordance with their individual Beings.

Some people teach that the Holy Spirit came upon Christ at His baptism and left Him at the time of the crucifixion. When we accept the unity of the Godhead, that teaching becomes impossible to accept. The Spirit could not come upon someone with whom He was eternally united. Hebrews 4:19 says it was through the Spirit that Christ offered Himself to God as an atonement for sin.

If a person came to you and said, "I know Christ saved me but I'm not sure God will keep me saved if I grieve the Holy Spirit," you would have an answer for them based on the Tri-unity of the Godhead. If Christ saved you then God saved you and the Spirit saved you. If Christ gave you eternal life then God is not going to take something away from you which He gave through the eternal Spirit.

Sometimes people try to draw practical lines between the persons of the Godhead. They might acknowledge that God inspired the Bible and specifically prohibited adultery. But in the same breath they might claim that they received a vision from the Holy Spirit in prayer telling them that in their case adultery was justified. Obviously a united, Triune God would not work in opposition to Himself. The Bible has given us all scripture "by inspiration of God" (II Timothy 3:16). The Holy Spirit has been One with God the Father and God the Son in that process and will never deny what He Himself has inspired. The Spirit will never disagree with the Word of God.

As you study the Word of God on which each of these DARES is based, and fill your notebook with truth about the attributes of God, remind yourself that everything you learn about God the Father is also true of God the Son and God the Holy Spirit.

Read through one the four Gospels. Every time you come to the words of Jesus, remind yourself that the words you are reading are the words of God. Remember that the actions of God the Son are the actions of God the Spirit and God the Father.

As you study passages in the Old Testament, remind yourself that all of the names of God such as Jehovah, Elohim and Adonai refer to all three Persons of the Tri-unity. Every act of God throughout the entire Bible is equally an act of Jesus and the Holy Spirit.

Study Ephesians 1:3-14, noting how the work of salvation is the work of the Tri-unity. God the Father, God the Son and God the Holy Spirit are all active participants in the one plan of salvation.

Dare Five

God, the Uncreated

"God said to Moses, "I am who I am. This is what
you are to say to the Israelites:
'I am has sent me to you'."
Exodus 3:14

"The most popular theory of our universe's
origin centers on a cosmic cataclysm unmatched in all
of history—the big bang," according to National
Geographic.

"Before the big bang, scientists believe, the
entire vastness of the observable universe, including
all of its matter and radiation, was compressed into a
hot, dense mass just a few millimeters across. This
nearly incomprehensible state is theorized to have

existed for just a fraction of the first second of time."
(nationalgeographic.com).

Scientists admit that this theory leaves several
questions unanswered. In the article cited above from
National Geographic, the main unanswered question
concerned the original cause of the big bang itself.
However, an even more fundamental question faces
the thinking mind. Where did the hot, dense mass
come from? To truly discuss origins it becomes
necessary to explore that question. Had the hot,
dense mass always existed? According to the article
it existed for only a fraction of a second before
exploding. So what caused it to exist for that fraction
of a second?

God, according to the Bible, is the source of
all things. While He created all things, He Himself is
the uncreated. He existed from eternity past and will
continue on into eternity future. And yet even that
description remains incomplete because there are no
limits with God. Eternity suggests time, and God
existed before time, which means He existed before
eternity.

"Origin is a word that can apply only to things
created. When we think of anything that has origin,

we are not thinking of God. God is self-existent, while all created things necessarily originated somewhere at some time. Aside from God, nothing is self-caused." (Tozer).

Human reasoning finds it difficult to conceive of God apart from time and space. We think of Him as dwelling in the temple in the Old Testament. We notice that He is present at the time of Biblical events. We understand that Jesus came to earth at the incarnation and will return at the time of the second coming. Because of those observations we think of God being in a certain place, or part of a certain object, or here at a certain time. While God does inhabit the time and space which He created, He exists apart from that time and space. He is not bound by either of them. There is no past, present or future in the mind of God except as He relates to His creation. No up or down, backward or forward, in or out, close or far away limits Him in any fashion.

Recent court cases involving the teaching of creation and evolution have centered on the teaching of "scientific creationism" as a science rather than theology. If we recognize God as the only Uncreated One it becomes impossible to arrive at a creation model without admitting that such a study includes theology. By the same token it becomes impossible to espouse an evolutionary viewpoint of origins without denying the existence of an originator, a Creator.

DARE to base your world view on the foundation of a belief in God as the Uncreated. As you study the Word and increase in your knowledge of Him, deliberately choose to focus on the fact that He is not limited by or dependent upon man or the rest of the universe in any way. If every particle or matter, all spatial relationships and time itself were to disappear, God would still be God, unchanged in essence.

Dare Six

God Who Needs Nothing

"For as the Father has life in himself, so he has
granted the Son also to have life in himself."
John 5:26

Henry Ward Beecher, a well-known preacher
from Boston, brought a sermon on Thanksgiving Day,
1860. "The southern states ... have organized society
around a rotten core,—slavery: the North has
organized society about a vital heart,—liberty....
They stand in proper contrast. God holds them up to
ages and to nations, that men may see the difference."

Southern preacher J. W. Tucker, preaching in
Fayetteville, North Carolina, in May of 1862 said
this. "Your cause is the cause of God, of Christ, of
humanity. It is a conflict of truth with error—of the

37

Bible with Northern infidelity—of a pure Christianity with Northern fanaticism—of liberty with despotism—of right with might." (Christianity Today).

During the history of Israel, the nation often entered into battle thinking God was on their side. All the time God was teaching them that He did not need them, they needed Him to fight for them. They never won a battle without His help. He never lost a battle even without their help.

One of the reasons the image of God we conceive in our minds is so weak is simply because we envision a God who is in need of help. We say we believe that God is Almighty, but we think He needs the help of human armies to accomplish His will. We view Him as sitting on His throne and wringing His hands over the results of a political election. We feed our egos by convincing ourselves that His work on earth absolutely cannot be done without the effort we put into our own ministries. At the same time, we conclude that everyone else is doing ministry wrongly, that God is on our side and it is our responsibility to malign and expose every person who approaches the spiritual life from a viewpoint other than our own.

"Again, God needs no defenders. He is the eternal Undefended. To communicate with us in an idiom we can understand, God in the Scriptures makes full use of military terms; but surely it was never intended that we should think of the throne of the Majesty on high as being under siege, with Michael and his hosts or some other heavenly beings defending it from stormy overthrow." (Tozer).

We take a stand for the truth because we know it is right, not because we think someone might prove God to be wrong unless we defend Him.

True apologetics, or defense of the faith, comes from a desire to see the blinded eyes of mankind open to the reality of God. Faith does not wait for tests of authenticity on the Shroud of Turin in order to accept the truth of the resurrection.

We carry the message of the gospel to the unsaved world, not because we think God could not save them without our aid, but because we are thrilled to be chosen by Him as ambassadors of His kingdom.

William Carey was once rebuked by an older minister with the suggestion that if God wanted to convert the heathen He could do it without the help of Carey. In your notebook record your response to that statement based on the fact that God needs nothing. Why is it wrong to reason from the self-sufficiency of God that since God does not need us He will not choose to use us and even reward us for obedience and service?

In your notebook write your thoughts about God in relationship to Philippians 2:12-13. "Therefore, my dear friends, as you have always obeyed—not only in my presence, but now much more in my absence—continue to work out your salvation with fear and trembling, for it is God who works in you to will and to act in order to fulfill his good purpose." (NIV). Why are we expected to work out our salvation when everything depends on God who works within us? How does a healthy spiritual life result from both the knowledge that God does not need us and the truth that He wants to use us to fulfill his purposes?

DARE to adore and serve a God who has life in Himself! A God who needs nothing, gives everything, accepts what we offer Him and rewards us for using the very gifts He has given.

Dare Seven

A Beautiful God

"One thing I ask from the Lord, this only do I
seek: that I may dwell in the house of the Lord all the
days of my life, to gaze on the beauty of the Lord and
to seek him in his temple."
Psalm 27:4

Contemporary music group Rend Collective

draws on this verse concerning the beauty of the Lord

in the lyrics to their song "Keep Me Near."

"You are everything that is beautiful
You are all that I long to see in me
You are everything that is beautiful
Breathe Your desires in me
Form in us a heart of divine beauty
Form in us a heart of divine beauty
Form in us a heart of divine beauty."

41

Traditional hymnody also calls on that imagery in the words of such songs as "Beautiful Savior" translated by Joseph Seiss from an unknown author who wrote in 1677.

> "Fair are the meadows,
> Fair are the woodlands,
> Robed in flowers of blooming spring;
> Jesus is fairer,
> Jesus is purer;
> He makes our sorrowing spirit sing."

Normally when we think of God as beautiful our minds go immediately to something material. Other religions have produced many beautiful images of the gods they choose to worship. However, the fact that the Law of Moses specifically forbade any "graven images" (Exodus 20:4) eliminates that possibility from our understanding of the beauty of the Lord described in Psalm 27:4. The fact that God is a Spirit also excludes a material expression of beauty from our understanding. No one has ever seen God. The psalmist must have something else in mind when he desires to gaze on God's beauty.

That is not to deny the fact that God has beauty. Beauty, like all His other attributes, is perfect and unlimited. It is only the way we think about that beauty which must be adjusted in order to increase our knowledge of God. Our minds must resist approaching God's beauty through human standards regarding color of hair, shape of a nose or height of cheekbones.

Bernhard Andersen suggests that references to gazing on the beauty of the Lord may refer to seeing the liturgical dramas in the temple which re-enacted and glorified the work of God. W. H. Bellinger agrees that such descriptions must be understood in the context of worship. The psalmist in another place encourages people to "Give unto the LORD the glory due unto his name; worship the LORD in the beauty of holiness" (Psalm 29:2 KJV).

Although we cannot see God in His beauty with our eyes, we can see God's beauty in our hearts of worship. We can contemplate His holiness, gaze in awe upon His majesty, and remember his loving-kindness. We can give Him glory as we think about His love, enjoy His fellowship in prayer, and rejoice in the revelation of Himself in His Word.

DARE to see the beauty of God in all His works. Exult in the unbounded compassion and care with which He prepared for our salvation through Jesus Christ. Explore the unending creativity of God through an observation of the use of color in the natural world. Give Him praise for the exceedingly complex and yet practical way He has crafted the bodies in which we live. Revel in the intricate design of His creation. Learn to see Him in the pattern of every leaf in your garden, the splash of every mountain stream, the stupendous power of the lightning strike, and the waft of the gentle breeze on a still summer day.

Prepare and post a visual feast from nature scenes which you enjoy, using public media. With each online post include the tag: "All beauty is God's beauty."

Join in corporate worship with every fiber of your being. God has granted us the privilege of worshipping through our own efforts to describe His beauty. Enjoy the songs and hymns, the drama and prayer, the architectural settings and visual symbols of His beauty men and women have used to help us gaze upon Him in appreciation of that which we cannot see with our eyes. Open your heart to the beauty of God.

Dare Eight

An Eternal God

"The eternal God is a dwelling place, and
underneath are the everlasting arms;"
Deuteronomy 33:27

Sidney Edward Mezes, former president of
City College of New York and a member of the
United States delegation to negotiate the Treaty of
Versailles, offered the following illustration to help
explain the concept of eternity.

"As if all of us were cylinders, with the ends
removed, moving through the waters of some placid
lake. To the cylinders the waters seem to move.
What has passed is a memory, what is to come is
doubtful. But the lake knows that all the water is
equally real, and that it is quiet, immovable,

unruffled. Speaking technically, time is no reality.
Things seem past and future, and, in a sense, non-
existent to us, but, in fact, they are just as genuinely
real as the present is." (*Systematic Theology*, Strong).

Understanding that God exists in eternity and
outside of time does not change the reality of time for
us. We have been created to live within the
constraints of time. Human activity must still be
based on what has happened in the past and what
might happen in the future. Our decisions today
affect our condition tomorrow because that is the way
God has created the universe and our interaction with
the rest of His creation.

God in His Word has chosen to reveal a
limited number of future events. Apart from that we
cannot predict the course of life in our time-bound
existence. We can remember the past and plan for the
future, but the only life available to us inhabits
present time. God is not like that at all. He has no
past, present or future. Choosing to interact with a
universe ruled by time, God still exists personally
beyond time constraints. It would be wrong to
describe Him as bound by time in any way. For
example, if we were to suggest that all of human
history is in the present for God we would be limiting

Him to a time descriptor. Instead we must simply accept the truth that God is eternal, totally unrestricted by time in any way.

Eternality may be one of the most difficult of all divine attributes to understand simply because the human mind finds it almost impossible to think in terms of anything other than time. Yesterday, today and tomorrow form the prism through which we view life. Yesterday, today and tomorrow are all the same to God. God knows "the end from the beginning" (Isaiah 46:10). The same divine mind which knew the exact activities surrounding the death of Christ and revealed those events to prophets years in advance, knows the specific incidents of human history which have not yet occurred.

The eternal nature of God's existence cannot simply be related to our time-bound thinking. That is, we cannot think of eternity as an attribute of God which affects only His knowledge. Every other attribute of God exists in perfect harmony with His eternality. He is unchangeable because He is eternal. The fact that He is eternal means that His love, grace, mercy, kindness, holiness and every other divine attribute is also eternal. Nothing that happens in time can change the One who has created time and in whom time lives. What we see as the events of human history do not change God in any fashion.

Our reaction to the fact that God is eternal can take many forms. Some would use that fact to approach life from a fatalistic world-view. They would argue that since God is unchangeable, life is unchangeable, and all we can do is grin and bear it. But that is not life as revealed in the Word. God created us as time-bound creatures in order to make it possible for us to make both current and eternal decisions in the light of our temporal existence. He has given us a past, present and future so that we can learn from the past, hope for the future and be wise in our present conduct.

DARE to discover the impact of God's eternality.

In your notebook record the words used in each of the following passages of Scripture to indicate the fact that God is eternal. Then return to each verse and record a practical application to your own life based on the fact that God is eternal.

Deuteronomy 32:40

Psalm 90:2

Psalm 102:27

Isaiah 41:4

I Corinthians 2:7

Ephesians 1:4

I Timothy 1:17

I Timothy 6:16

Revelation 1:8

John 1:1

Jude 25

Hebrews 1:8

Dare Nine

An Infinite God

"Heaven and the heaven of heavens cannot
contain thee."
I Kings 8:27

Artist Maurits Cornelis Escher created some
of the world's most famous explorations of infinity.
He excelled in the graphic arts with impossible
constructions such as "Ascending and Descending."
In that piece a set of stairs winds through a palace.
Allowing your eye to follow it either in ascent or
descent you eventually find yourself right back where
you started.

The concept of illustrating infinity with a
closed topology occurs also in the theories of some

cosmologists. They would argue that the surface of a globe such as one of the planets has no edge and yet it is finite. Traveling in a straight line around a globe would bring you back to where you started similar to Escher's drawing. A seemingly infinite universe could have a similar topology. If a person traveled through a boundless universe for a long enough period of time, it might be discovered that the curvature of the universe would bring you back to the very place from which you started.

Whether in Mathematics, Logic, Cosmology, or the Arts, the concept of infinity has provided material for endless speculation and discussion. Biblical theology takes another step beyond such discussions to posit a God who, having created a universe which spatially may go on forever, has an existence outside of the space which He created. The infinity of God relates to physical space in the same way the eternity of God relates to temporal time. God created space but is not bound by that space in any fashion. He inhabits the space He created, but also exists outside of any spatial relationships. While everywhere present, He cannot be said to be contained in any object or confined to any geographical location.

Descriptions of God in relation to the physical world fall into the same category as anthropomorphisms. Anthropomorphism describes non-human entities in terms of human characteristics. We know that God is Spirit, possessing no body. When the scripture describes the hands of God or the feet of God we understand the metaphor without concluding that He actually possesses hands or feet. In the same way, when we read that God dwells in the Tabernacle we understand that such a description does not require a physical presence within a structure or a confinement of an infinite God to a spatial existence. He dwells in the Tabernacle while being everywhere else at the same time.

The immensity of God can certainly be postulated from the size of the expanding universe, but it would be wrong to conclude that the size of the universe limits the size of God in any way. Yet even in writing such a sentence using the word size we have placed a human limitation on God. Infinity cannot be defined in terms of size or it would not be infinite. Infinity must be conceived in terms which exist outside of space, and human language seems almost incapable of describing a non-spatial concept. The best we have come up with is the lemniscate or infinity symbol ∞. Yet it must be noted that even in this symbol the solution to infinity involves returning to the place you started.

Contemplating the infinity of God will quickly lead a believer to the conclusion that the concept of a spatially limitless God will never be completely understood. But a lack of understanding does not mean this attribute has no personal value for us. The very fact that only God possesses infinity leads us to a position of tremendous personal confidence in Him. The created universe is not infinite, so deterioration and decay of the environment does not indicate a diminishing of His power. Sin is not infinite, so the exponential growth of sin cannot change the redemptive plan for the forgiveness of sin accomplished by an infinite God. Satan is not infinite, so we need not accept some theory of a battle between good and evil or between the light and the dark side which may somehow be lost by the Lord's armies. God controls time and space. He dwells outside of time and space. Nothing and no one inhabiting time and space can affect His infinity in any way. He is "before all things and in him all things hold together" (Colossians 1:17).

Infinitude should not be thought of in spatial terms. God's infinity is not like a huge rubber band which needs to be stretched in order to cover everything. We must not think of Him in terms of an infinite number of snowflakes covering the universe. God's presence in all His completeness permeates all of creation, yet He is not limited or defined by space in any way. God chooses to occupy the time and space He created, but He transcends them both.

The practical application of God's infinity lies in its relationship to all the rest of His attributes. DARE to apply the truth of His infinity to everything else He has revealed concerning His own Person. In your notebook consider the following questions in relation to the amazing truth of the infinity of God.

1. Is the love of God stretched thin in order for Him to love the world?
2. Is God's love divided among humanity so that one person receives a greater or smaller portion than someone else?

3. Is the holiness of God stretched thin in order to cover all who have been forgiven?

4. Is the wisdom of God divided so that some parts of the universe suffer from His neglect?

5. Is the mercy of God offered in a greater portion to certain parts of the creation?

6. Is the availability of God's grace dependent on the locale where a person lives?

7. Is the strength of God diminished when natural disasters occur in rapid succession?

8. Is the longsuffering of God present toward those in one part of the world and absent from other locations?

9. Are some people more deserving of God's salvation because they live in a country with a history of religious practice?

10. Is there any place in the entire universe where a person can escape from the presence of an infinite God?

Dare Ten

God Who Never Changes

"Every good gift and every perfect gift is from
above, and cometh down from the Father of
lights, with whom is no variableness,
neither shadow of turning."
James 1:17

According to the American Academy of
Dermatology, each one of us possesses about nineteen
million skin cells to every square inch. The tops layer
of our skin is composed of dead cells, and we slough
off 30,000 to 40,000 of those every day. By the end
of one month, the skin showing right now will be
completely replaced.

Our bodies are in a state of constant flux. The world around us changes constantly, passing through seasons of the year, temperature fluctuations, and the effects of human progress from building construction to cutting lawns.

In stark contrast to the change which accompanies every aspect of human life stands a God who never changes. James uses the word "perfect" (James 1:17) to describe God's gifts. The word can also be used to describe the Giver of the gifts. When something or someone is perfect there can be no improvement. If improvement were possible it would not be perfect. There can be no change for the worse because that would also destroy perfection. God cannot change because He is altogether perfect.

One of the mysteries of the incarnation, or God taking upon Himself flesh, involves this matter of change. As a man Jesus Christ grew and developed. He lost skin cells just as we all do. He lost baby teeth and changed shoe sizes. He "grew in wisdom and stature" (Luke 2:52). Completely man, He experienced change, and completely God, he changed nothing. "Jesus Christ is the same yesterday and today and forever" (Hebrews 13:8). Being changeless does not limit God's activity. He remained changeless in His divine nature while acting on behalf of men through every change of human existence, including death.

Since God never changes, what He says never changes. What He said to Moses and David, He says to us. We may change in our understanding of the Word of God, but there has never been and will never be any change in what He has given us by revelation.

The truth concerning God's changelessness must be our reassurance when we fail to control the change in the world around us. We live in a world in chaos where change becomes the norm. As believers we may find that frustrating, simply because the changes always seem to move in the direction of sin rather than righteousness. What mankind once accepted as good can quickly become the new evil, light becomes darkness and darkness becomes light. When that happens we must accept the fact that things have changed while clinging tightly to the unchanging character of God.

Changelessness must never be confused with immobility. The fact that He does not change will never limit the power of God and should not be reduced to an impersonal Fate or Karma. God remains constantly active in nature and on behalf of mankind with every action in accordance with His unchanging essence. God was no different after creation than He was before. His grace during the church age does not differ from the grace He displayed in the days of the Law. His wisdom has not increased during the age of technology. Human philosophers have contributed nothing to His understanding.

The fact that man is capable of change brings joy to the heart when we consider the matter of salvation. Once at enmity with God, we can repent of sin and become the friend of God. The repentance marks a change in us and not in Him. Instead of going our own way we have changed direction and now travel in companionship with Him. He has not changed, but our ways have become His ways.

DARE to live in acceptance of the unchangeableness of God. Be willing to give up any attempt to control your own future and trust that future to God. Avoid despair resulting from the changing chaos in the world around us, resting instead on the confidence we can have in a God who changes not.

Make a list of all the changes which have taken place in your life over the past twelve months. Include personal experiences and physical differences as well as shifts in economics, politics, morals, relationships and beliefs in the world around us. Head a second column on your page with the word GOD and beside every change in the first column write UNCHANGED.

DARE to worship and exalt God for that word UNCHANGED. No matter what we face in life, we can face it and not fear when we trust a God who never changes.

Dare Eleven

God Immaterial

"The Son is the image of the invisible God,
the firstborn over all creation."
Colossians 1:15

When Yuri Gagarin, the first Russian
cosmonaut, returned from his historical journey into
space in 1961, reports widely reported him saying
that he did not see God in space. Actually, the words
were never a part of his official conversations with
Earth at any time during his spaceflight. Instead they
may have originated within a speech given by Nikita
Khrushchev before the Central Committee some time
later, insisting that Gagarin had traveled into space
and had not seen God. (Pravmir.com).

If Gagarin had seen God it would have been far greater news than Khrushchev's claim which he made to support the official Soviet line of atheism. The Bible clearly states that "no one has ever seen God" (John 1:18). The reason for that is quite simple—God exists without any material essence which could be seen by human eyes. His being is not composed of matter and has no connection with anything material. After all, the material world came into existence at the time of creation and God, being eternal, existed long before anything material had been formed.

Any description of God which speaks of a face or hands or feet must be understood as His determination to describe the unimaginable in anthropomorphic terms comprehensible to the human mind. Appearances of God in the Old Testament demonstrate His ability to temporarily take on human form in order to interact with His creatures, but they in no way negate the specific declarations of Scripture concerning his existence as Spirit (cf. John 4:24).

As humans we possess the imaginative capacity to conceive of the immaterial. Love, for example, has no material existence and yet has become the favorite subject of art and literature. The danger in bringing to life the immaterial through imagination lies in the tendency to assume that the creation of our minds composes the totality of what we have imagined. Describing God as "the man upstairs" limits His omnipresence by confining Him to a certain geographical location. But there were undoubtedly those who likewise limited Him geographically to dwelling in the temple, ignoring His presence in all of His creation and creating in their own imaginations a local deity.

Our every thought about God, including an investigation of His attributes, must constantly avoid limiting Him in any way. Talented musicians have described Him in lyrics which soar with praise, but we must never think that our meager attempts at worship liturgies in any way begin to compare with the transcendence of His Being. Magnificent cathedrals elevate our minds and produce awesome emotions of divine ascendency which crown Him with glory and honor, but edifices of stone will never contain the immaterial. Artistic masterpieces awaken within our very souls an appreciation of the perfection of deity, but fail to truly represent even the corner of His garment.

DARE to revel in the imaginative expansiveness of knowing an immaterial God. Life, so bound with and bounded by the material, disappears into an eternal existence of communion with the spiritual, the immaterial. Heaven itself, so often limited in our minds to the gloriously familiar mansions over the hilltop and streets of gold, morphs out of the material into a glorious effulgence of the unimaginable. Pure light. Pure love. Pure spirit. Pure holiness. Pure joy.

Choose one of the following:

> The greatest painting ever created.
> The most magnificent building ever constructed.
> The outstanding musical composition of all time.
> The most beautiful sight in the natural world.

Focus your mind on the subject you have chosen and think of ways it could be even greater. Destroy all limits of time and space, cost and availability of materials, size and location. If possible allow your imagination to soar from what is seen to that which is unseen, the very essence of what your subject represents, the immaterial of which it is the symbol. When the outer limits of your human imagination have been strained beyond belief, DARE to say to yourself— "God is yet beyond. The very best my imagination can create comes only from the shadow of the invisible God. I have dared and only begun to catch a small glimpse of the God transcendent. But I have walked on water."

Dare Twelve

God is Life

"But the Lord is the true God;
he is the living God, the eternal King."
Jeremiah 10:10

NOVA conducted an interview for PBS with Andrew Knoll, a professor of biology at Harvard, concerning the subject of life and its beginnings. Knoll defines life as a "system that's capable of Darwinian evolution." By that he means an arrangement of protein and nucleic acids which can grow and reproduce with variations. When asked directly how life got going on the Earth he says, "The short answer is we really don't know." Professor Knoll proceeds to offer a number of suggestions concerning how life may have originated and then concludes with this statement, "I imagine my grandchildren will still be sitting around saying that it's a great mystery, but that they will understand that mystery at a level that would be incomprehensible today." (Knoll, NOVA).

What evolutionary scientists acknowledge as a great mystery finds a simple and yet profound solution in scripture. "In Him was life," (John 1:4). Some scientists see an eternal inanimate existence which at some point in time becomes animate, able to grow and reproduce. The Bible describes an eternal Being, one with intellect, emotion and will, although immaterial, who does not need to grow because He is perfect, but chooses to reproduce through creation a universe of time, space, and matter. Within that universe He places both the animate and the inanimate. He gives physical life to the plant and animal kingdoms and both physical life and the capability of spiritual life to humanity. A. H. Strong says, "The total life of the universe is only a faint image of that moving energy which we call the life of God."

We can begin to understand the life of God by comparison and contrast. Rocks have existence without life and are incapable of motion in themselves. Water moves when acted upon by gravity but cannot be said to possess life. Plants remain stationary while rooted to the ground but do give evidence of life through growth and reproduction. Animal life possesses sensitive powers such as seeing, hearing and smelling while performing the functions of life such as sleeping, eating, walking and reproducing. Human life exists on a higher plane than all of those previous forms of life with ability to reason, emote and choose rather than being controlled by simple instinct. No creature apart from man has ever composed a symphony, written a novel or built a skyscraper.

As great a gap as exists between the fully developed life of man and the existence of rocks and minerals, an even greater distance separates life as we know it from the life which God possesses. All life in the universe depends on outside forces. Ultimately that force is God, but even within the realm of daily subsistence, offspring owe their very existence to parents. In contrast to that reality God owes His existence to nothing. His essence is life. The fact of His eternality demands a life without cause or dependence on any other. Were God dependent on someone other for life He would be less than perfect and cease to be God.

Human life involves a combination of soul and body, and when the soul departs the body may look the same but is recognized to be dead. Divine life involves no such combination of parts. The attribute of Unity in God stands incapable of division as evidenced in other attributes such as infinity, perfection, all-sufficiency and immutability.

No other is in any way like God. He alone possesses life and He alone can give life to any other. Plant life comes from God so it is proper to give Him thanks for the abundance of sustenance received from seasons of sowing, growing and harvest. Animal life exists because He gives life and breath. The provision of meat for eating, beasts of burden, pets for companionship and the enjoyment of viewing animal life in the wild should produce in each one of us a sense of immense gratitude to the God of creation.

Every advancement attained by modern man originated in the creative mind of God who gave the human race intelligence, the ability to communicate, logical thought and the insatiable quest for knowledge. Physical life and all of the adventure of living comes to us as a gift from the Giver of life.

Spiritual life, available to every person who ever lived or will live, likewise owes its existence to the grace, mercy, love and foresight of Almighty God. Aware that man would fall into sin, God planned even before creation to quicken those who were dead in sin. Through the death and resurrection of the Son of God, salvation was made available to all who would call upon Him. When a person places faith in the finished work of Christ, God grants them His own righteousness, justifies them in His sight and grants them a new life—the life of Christ. New life makes possible a transformed existence on this earth and guarantees eternal life in heaven. The giving of spiritual life, the living of spiritual life, and the enjoyment of eternal spiritual life emanate from and depend entirely upon the life which is in God.

DARE to expand your insight into the vastness of the life of God. Granted, we can only think human thoughts, but even so it should be possible for us to imagine things greater than what we have experienced.

Start by comparing the life (existence) of a rock to that of a tree. List every comparison you can think of which demonstrates the superiority of life as a tree over life as a rock. Next do the same with the tree and an animal such as a beautiful stallion. What advantages will a stallion possess in comparison to the tree? The third step would compare human life to that of the horse. Here you could spend immense amounts of time. The horse will never go to college, never write a poem, never search the Internet, never know love and never have a spiritual relationship with God.

Now make a list of some of the latest inventions and advancements of the human race. These might include nanobots, liquid optical lenses, the hoverboard, bionic ears and the latest Ipad modifications. Choosing one or several of those achievements, allow your mind to imagine how much greater that technology might become through the power of an unlimited God who possesses and can grant life.

Finally, compare the latest inventions of humanity to the creative accomplishments of Almighty God. Man may invent an artificial heart, but God made exactly the heart needed to keep man alive. Make a list of as many innovations as possible and recognize that all of them depend on the material universe God created. Man has life because God gave him life. Mankind has intellect, emotion and will because that is the way God made us.

DARE to enjoy your foray into the potential accomplishments of the God of life. Above all, dare to enjoy Him—and through Him the life He gives.

Dare Thirteen

A God Who Knows All

"Oh, the depth of the riches and wisdom and
knowledge of God! How unsearchable are his
judgments and how inscrutable his ways!"
Romans 11:33

The Pacific Magazine reprinted the following

anonymous poem from the Montreal Daily Star titled

"Father and I."

> "My father and I know everything
> In the whole wide world, we do!"
> My little son nodded his curls at me;
> "Just everything, Mother—true."
> "Then tell me, Sir Bragg," I teasing said,
> "Where in the world so wide
> I can find the country of Yucatan?"
> He answered with unmoved pride.
> "That one is Father's to tell—it's hard.
> The easies are mine. But we

> Together know all that there is to know.
> Ask one that belongs to me."

The trust a young boy places in the knowledge of his father provides an apt comparison to the trust we can place in the omniscience of God. Perfect and complete knowledge of all things past, present and future means that God is never surprised. What a comfort such knowledge can bring to the life of a believer. He knows when people lie about us. We never have to convince Him that malicious gossip is wrong. He knows when we have sinned and still stands ready to forgive. He knows what we fear, why we fail and what grieves us about our own decisions.

It is also true that God is never shocked. That does not mean He approves of every act of mankind, but it removes an important barrier to confession. We need not fear His rejection when we tell Him what is in our hearts. He already knows.

God's omniscience involves both the actual and the possible. He knows what we could have made of our lives, what we have made of our lives and what we can yet make of our lives. He knows what is best for us and always works through His Word to guide us into that path.

As with so many of God's attributes, some popular misconceptions have arisen concerning omniscience. Some people think that God knows all things but that He can forget. They believe that if enough time passes God will forget their sin. Others assume that God does not care or is not paying attention. Pride can lead a person to the conclusion that he knows more than God.

DARE to live in the light of God's perfect knowledge. Trust Him to lead you in the right paths. Never forget that He cares and is working in every way to change you into the very best person you can be, one in sync with the character of His own Son.

Dare to explore the scriptures to see what God knows. In describing the omniscience of God the Bible lists many instances of things which are objects of His knowledge. Look up the following verses and write down in your notebook the things which these verses tell us God knows.

> Psalm 147:4
>
> Matthew 10:29-30
>
> Psalm 33:13-15
>
> Acts 15:8
>
> Psalm 139:2

Matthew 6:8

Isaiah 46:9-10

Dare Fourteen

God All-Wise

"To the only wise God be glory forever
through Jesus Christ! Amen."
Romans 16:27

The possibility of obtaining knowledge
without wisdom has been enshrined in the popular
mind by the stereotype of the absent-minded
professor. Disney created a classic example in the
1961 movie of the same name, starring Fred
MacMurray. Professor Ned Brainard invents flying
rubber which he dubs Flubber. Ned becomes so
excited about his discovery that he misses his own
wedding for the third time, hence the absent-minded
designation. Even though a genius in his own right

81

and the inventor of a marvelous discovery, Ned Brainard does not always possess the wisdom to use his knowledge effectively.

God not only possesses unlimited knowledge, or omniscience, He also demonstrates total wisdom in all His thoughts and actions. Like all of God's attributes, wisdom works in correlation with every other attribute. Imagine in science fiction a large brain in a container, hooked up to life-giving resources, but without a body. That would picture wisdom without might. Such a brain would be totally dependent on others to work out the plans he conceives. The wisdom of God, accompanied by the power of God, can achieve everything the mind of God decides to do.

Like our study of all the truth concerning God, we must begin with the knowledge we already possess. Human wisdom becomes our starting point, and we may well marvel at the advances in technology, astronomy, the life sciences and medicine over the past decades. The knowledge of man increases exponentially and wise men have accomplished great things. But even to use the word "increase" demonstrates the vast chasm between the wisdom of man and the wisdom of God. There will never be an increase in God's wisdom. He will never need to publish a new edition of His textbook. Discovery will never be a part of His vocabulary.

Perfect wisdom includes both the ability to decide what should be done and to do what should be done. There can be no flaw in a wisdom that flows from perfect knowledge. There can be no fault in the means to that end wrought by Omniscience. "The testimony of faith is that, no matter how things look in this fallen world, all God's acts are wrought in perfect wisdom." (Tozer, The Knowledge of the Holy).

One of the greatest difficulties men face when they contemplate the wisdom of God involves the existence of evil and sorrow in our world. We think that we could improve on the way things work in this world if given the chance. The truth is that given the opportunity which faced Adam and Eve every one of us would have made the same choice to disobey. The fact that God gave mankind free will and allowed the human race to fall into sin does not diminish His wisdom. The evil choices of men and women cannot be blamed on Him. Instead the destructive consequences of sinful choices should be viewed as one of the ways in God's wisdom we are shown our need of salvation.

Pain from a broken leg drives even the person who hates hospitals the most to seek medical help. A doctor may initiate even more pain in setting the bone so that it will heal properly. We would not blame the doctor for the initial break and even though we may resent the pain he causes we realize that the result of his wisdom will be best for our future. Viewing life through the wisdom of God helps us see that even pain has a purpose when it shows us the need for divine help.

DARE to view the events of your life through the lens of God's wisdom. Rather than becoming bitter or falling into despair because of difficult times, ask yourself how the unfailing wisdom of God can work through you in the face of those circumstances to produce an inner character "thoroughly equipped for every good work" (II Timothy 3:16 NIV).

Write an ending to each of the following scenes, imagining how the "trial of your faith" (I Peter 1:7) could bring about spiritual improvement in your life through the wisdom of God.

1. Downsizing has begun to affect the company for whom you work. In order to keep a job similar to the one you have done for the past fifteen years you will need to uproot your family and move to a new town. You really hate the thought of leaving your church which you love, and initial investigation reveals that no similar church exists in the community to which you will be moving. What might God in His wisdom be daring you to do?

2. Having just celebrated your twenty-fifth wedding anniversary you are shocked by the medical evaluation giving your spouse less than six months to live. You have prayed for a miracle and are seeking to trust God, but if the prayer for healing is not answered can there still be a future path for you to walk with God? What might God in His wisdom have in store for one who dares to trust Him in death's valley?

3. A misunderstanding of your intentions and goals for the future has brought to an end the ministry to which you have dedicated your life. You are convinced that certain persons, jealous of your success, have manipulated and even lied to turn leadership against you. Determined not to respond in kind you have

decided to simply walk away from your dreams. What might God in His wisdom dare you to do in the years to come?

Dare Fifteen

God Our Refuge

"God is our refuge and strength, an ever-
present help in trouble."
Psalm 46:1

Children of the Cold War era still remember
those drills when we would take refuge under our
desks when the alarm sounded, as ridiculous as it was
to think that a school desk would protect us from an
atom bomb. But many others from those days
invested in far more serious forms of refuge. Fallout
shelters and their construction became a big business,
encouraged by various government agencies
including the Federal Civil Defense Administration.
"According to civil defense authorities, a concrete

block basement shelter could be built as a do-it-yourself project for $150 to $200. Exactly how much protection they actually afforded was an open question—one that, thankfully, no one has had to test, yet." (nebraskastudies.org).

The need for a fallout shelter came from the tremendous fear of nuclear war. That fear extended from families desiring to be safe from the bomb to entire nations. The United States and Russia, in particular, recognized the possibility that nuclear war would devastate both countries. A strategic military policy based on that possibility of mutually assured destruction, or MAD, became a major part of the defense policy of both nations.

When the psalmist rejoiced in the fact that God was a refuge, his thoughts also went immediately to the subject of fear. "Therefore will we not fear, though the earth give way and the mountains fall into the heart of the sea" (Psalm 46:2). Knowing God as our refuge protects us from fear. Knowing God may not keep us away from falling mountains or even nuclear war, as believers we can still face every situation without fear by hiding in Him. Nothing can keep us away from Him.

If we take our refuge in our stock portfolio we will live in fear of a market collapse. If our place of shelter from fear depends on a relationship, we will fear betrayal. Using drugs or alcohol as a refuge may bring escape from reality, but it will engender fear of destroyed health. A hiding place like a bomb shelter may have promised some protection from nuclear fallout, but it did nothing to lessen the fear of war.

Only God can provide a perfect refuge from fear. We need not fear death because in Him we have eternal life. We don't need to fear betrayal because His love is endless. Being lonely or abandoned will not be a fear when we have Him always at our side. Guilt need not be feared when we know His forgiveness. Fear of slander and gossip disappears when we remember that He knows the truth in every situation. Physical danger from floods or fires or tornados may damage our possessions and our very bodies, but even those can do nothing to separate us from God.

DARE to flee to God for refuge. The Apostle Paul expanded on this truth in the eighth chapter of the book of Romans, providing a specific list of events incapable of separating us from the "love of

Christ" (Romans 8:35). Transfer that list from Romans 8 into your notebook. Then, alongside each word used by Paul, write your own words to describe the specific fears from which God will protect you in His refuge.

Trouble

Hardship

Persecution

Famine

Nakedness

Peril

Sword

Death

Life

Angels

Demons

Present

Future

Any power

Height

Depth

Anything else in all creation

Dare Sixteen

God Our Joy

"Do not grieve, for the joy of the Lord
is your strength"
Nehemiah 8:10

One of the happiest scenes in classical literature occurs on the Christmas morning when Ebenezer Scrooge realizes the ghostly visitors have done their work all in one night. Waking in his own bed he rejoices to hear the church bells ringing in the blessed morn. "I am light as a feather, I am as happy as an angel, I am as merry as a school-boy," he exclaims. And then he laughs for the first time in many a year, a laugh which Dickens calls "The father of a long, long line of brilliant laughs." (Dickens, A Christmas Carol).

God is a God of pure, unending joy. Certainly we rejoice in Him, happy because of all He has done for us. But joy is not just an emotion we feel toward God, it is a part of His very character.

Consider some of the biblical descriptions God has shared with us concerning His joy.

Jesus told His disciples that He shared truth with them so that "my joy may be in you and that your joy may be complete" (John 15:11). In doing that He let them know that joy was a part of His divine nature and that only in Him would they ever find complete joy.

Paul wrote to the church in Galatia concerning the fruit of the Spirit, reminding them that the third Person of the Trinity possesses "joy" (Galatians 5:22) which He wants God's people to share.

In I Chronicles 16:27 we learn that "splendor and majesty are before Him, strength and joy are in His place." (NASB). Joy was in the place of God, the temple, because God Himself was there and where God was there was joy. No wonder David wrote, "I was glad when they said to me, 'Let us go to the house of the Lord'." (Psalm 122:1 NASB).

When the exiles returned to Jerusalem and celebrated the rebuilding of the temple they wept over their sin at the reading of the Law. But Nehemiah reminded them that even in their repentance and grief they had reason to rejoice, not because of their own joy but because of the joy of the Lord which would give them strength (cf. Neh. 8:10).

At the time of creation we learn that "the morning stars sang together and all the sons of God shouted for joy" (Job 38:7 NASB). Although the verse does not specifically describe the joy of God, we can certainly assume that if the angels were joyful it was a reflection of His own spirit.

When God gives victory to His people, His own reaction is to "exult over you with joy. He will be quiet in his love, He will rejoice over you with shouts of joy" (Zephaniah 3:17 NASB). When God delivers His people, He does it with great joy. His heart rejoices over the opportunity to bring victory on behalf of His own.

When Christ shared the parable of talents, a story where the master He describes is obviously

God, He says that the faithful servant was told to "enter into the joy of your master" (Matthew 25:23 NASB). Jesus Himself taught that joy is one of the characteristics by which God is known.

When a sinner accepts the Lord and finds salvation "there is joy in the presence of the angels of God" (Luke 15:10). And who is in the presence of the angels of God but God Himself? The salvation of the sinner brings forth a great expression of His personal joy.

When the disciples in the book of Acts received the filling of the Holy Spirit they were also filled with "joy" (Acts 13:52), suggesting that the presence of the Spirit in their lives brought with it a divine joy.

Joy must be seen as one of the innate characteristics of God, and since we are to become like Him through the indwelling Christ and the work of the Holy Spirit we should be people of joy as well. God is happy, and He wants us to be happy. Since He is the origin and source of joy, we can know true joy and happiness only through Him. Knowing God and serving Him will bring His joy into our lives.

Ignoring God and disobeying Him will produce joylessness and unhappiness.

DARE to mirror the joy of God in your own life. Take a selfie with the largest smile on your face which you can manage. Enlarge it to at least an 8 x 10 and tape it next to the mirror you use each morning. On the picture write: God's smile is my smile. Challenge yourself each time you see the picture to live that day in the joy of the Lord.

Dare Seventeen

God Our Song

"The LORD is my strength and song, and He
has become my salvation;
This is my God, and I will praise Him; My
father's God, and I will extol Him."
Exodus 15:2

G. F. Handel's Oratorio "Messiah," composed
in an amazing twenty-four days, is considered by
many to be the greatest musical composition ever
written. Charles Jennens took the words for the
Oratorio entirely from scripture and is said to have
voiced his hope that "Handel's music would be good
enough to accompany the words from the Bible."
(Payne and Lenzo, "The Handel's Messiah Family
Advent Reader"). Crowded auditoriums from its
premier and right down to today would agree that
Jennen's hope was realized.

97

From the beginning music has been closely associated with the worship of God. From the songs of creation (Job 38:7) to the Song of Moses (Exodus 15), from the songs of Zechariah and Mary (Luke 1:46-55, 67-79) to the Song of the Lamb (Revelation 15:3), music has been part of the relationship between God and His people. Though each of these scriptural examples provides us with lyrics, it is interesting to note that the word translated "song" in Exodus 15:2 actually has the sense of "melody" in the Hebrew. Our lyrics in worship glorify the majesty of God, but in a very real sense He Himself is the melody, the music, the song.

Accepting God as the Creator of music poses no difficulty for the spiritual mind which sees everything as crafted by His hand. But considering music as part of the very nature of God leads us a step further into our knowledge of Him. Seeing God as our Song pushes the origin of music back from the dawn of creation to infinitude. Forever God has been the Song. His gift of music to humanity becomes, like intellect, emotion and will, one of the qualities of His own being partially shared with men by virtue of the fact that we have been made in His image. The fall has certainly singed those attributes as sin twists them to its own devices. Intellect has become the tool of the agnostic. Emotion twists morality into lust in much of modern literature. Free will bends to the allurement of sinful pride and revels in disobedience to God. Like each of those, music often denigrates and debases humanity and deity instead of promoting holiness in the human heart and glory to God.

But the fact remains that the image of God in man, renewed through the life of our "mortal bodies through His Spirit, who lives in you" (Romans 8:11), proves capable of awesome achievement through the intellect, emotion and will which mirrors His image. Acknowledging God as our Song should convince us to see that same potential in music. Not just the lyrics taken from scripture, but the very melody, harmony and rhythm of "Messiah" proved capable of portraying the glory of the Lord.

> One beat only making time.
> Silence. Pregnant pause. Sublime
> Foresight. Then the birth of future.
> Present sewn to past. The suture
> Silken thread of sound igniting
> Music. Heaven and earth uniting.
>
> Morning stars with voice aligning
> Mystic melody. Heaven delighting

Consonance. Syncing with rhythmic choices.
Glissando blending seraphic voices.
A score, on score, composition divine,
Threads of infinitude sweetly entwine.

Glory revealed in symphonic assonance.
Sun, moon, star blaze with lightning
      extravagance.
Premiere performance, opening night,
Every musician a rank neophyte.
Triune production, fantasia's debut.
Theosmusica comes! Quiescence adieu.
        Allen, "Theosmusica"

DARE to discover God through Song.

1. Prepare a playlist on Spotify, iTunes, Google Play or iHeart Radio. Use that list for your personal listening for an entire week.

2. Augment your listening by obtaining a copy of a hymnal from your church or Christian bookstore. Read the lyrics as you would a devotional. Allow the melodies to permeate your subconscious so they become the soundtrack for your very existence.

3. Listen again to Handel's "Messiah" and other great classical music written for the glory of God. God has gifted many with the ability to honor His greatness through song. Use the music of the centuries to open your eyes to the unlimited, unimaginable, eternal existence of the magnificent God of Song.

Dare Eighteen

God Transcendent

"This was the appearance of the likeness of
the glory of the Lord. When I saw it, I fell
facedown, and I heard the voice of one
speaking."
Ezekiel 1:28

The video game "Transcendence" challenges
a player to experience a space adventure in the
farthest reaches of the universe. "Compelled to
journey to the Galactic Core by a mysterious
hyperintelligence, you must fight your way through
dozens of star systems teeming with clashing empires,
expansionist AIs, and fearsome xenophobes."
(store.steampowered.com).   Even with the promise of
Artificial Intelligence, and even hyperintelligence, the
game still occurs in the realm of human space.

The very definition of transcendence demonstrates the human inadequacy of language in applying such a word to a gaming encounter played within the finite reaches of human space. Transcendence describes something lying beyond the ordinary, something outside human perception. Transcendence "comes from the Latin prefix *trans-*, meaning 'beyond,' and the word *scandare,* meaning 'to climb'." (vocabulary.com). To climb beyond involves a condition outside of physical space and human reality, a position in reality belonging only to God.

Using human language to describe divine reality often leads us to such intellectual cul-de-sacs. A transcendent God exists beyond the limits of any of our physical senses. He cannot be seen with human eyes. He cannot be heard by human ears. We cannot smell Him, taste Him or touch Him. Only when He condescends to take upon Himself a form recognizable to those senses do we even begin to grasp with our poor minds a scintilla of awareness that He exists.

Even an encounter with the transcendence of God adapted to our human sensory organs was enough to bring Abraham to a prostrate position (cf. Genesis 17:3). Jacob saw God in a dream and woke with fear exclaiming "Surely the Lord is in this place, and I was not aware of it" (Genesis 28:16). Job confessed that he had been willing to argue with God when having only heard of Him, but when he saw Him he said, "I despise myself and repent in dust and ashes" (Job 42:6). The Apostle John had seen Jesus the Son of God in the flesh during His incarnation. But when He saw Him on the isle of Patmos appearing in heavenly glory he "fell at his feet as though dead" (Revelation 1:17).

"Forever God stands apart, in light unapproachable. He is as high above an archangel as above a caterpillar, for the gulf that separates the archangel from the caterpillar is but finite, while the gulf between God and the archangel is infinite." (Tozer, The Knowledge of the Holy).

The danger of losing a sense of the transcendence of God lies in moving Him from a position beyond to one which is near at hand. God has chosen to speak to our race through the process of inspiration, but to assume that we have heard the voice of God apart from the inspired Word of God degrades the very concept of a transcendent God who cannot be heard by human ears. Claiming to have seen God in any form likewise reduces Him to that which can be perceived by visual means. Feeling the hand of God upon us may be one way of describing a spiritual experience, but alleging the experience of having received a literal touch from God, healing or otherwise, demeans our appreciation of the One who is wholly Other.

DARE to consciously remove from your mind any image of God which reduces Him to a plane on a level equal to any part of His creation. That would obviously include the crafting and worship of idols, but it could also relate to the language we use in reference to God. Record yourself in a situation where you are praying in public. Check to see if you tend to use the words "Lord" or "God" in a manner which reduces them to space fillers rather than reverential terms of address. Consciously avoid flippancy, undue familiarity, and cliché phrases when communicating with the One whose name is majestic "in all the earth! You have set your glory in the heavens" (Psalm 8:1). Like those of old who saw the Lord, use a prone position for private prayer, demonstrating by your very physical humility the tremendous disparity existing between man and our transcendent God.

Dare Nineteen

God is Light

"In him was life, and that life was the light of men. The light shines in the darkness, but the darkness has not understood it."
John 1:4-5

The Olympic Cauldron and its pedestal always become one of the central focal points of the various Olympic venues. In Atlanta in 1996 the cauldron was an artistic scroll decorated in red and gold. Muhammed Ali used a mechanical, self-propelling fuse ball that transported the flame up a wire to light the cauldron during the opening ceremonies. Once lit, the flame could be seen burning over the stadium day and night.

Imagine not one great Olympic flame, but sixteen. Transport yourself back to a time when those sixteen torches burning in large cauldrons of oil did not have to compete with any other lights. When the golden bowls of oil were lit on top of the temple mount at the end of the feast of Tabernacles, they illuminated all of Jerusalem. Jesus stood in front of those sixteen cauldrons and proclaimed, "I am the light of the world" (John 8:12).

John uses the description of Christ as light sixteen times in his gospel. At the very beginning of chapter one he says "In him was life, and the life was the light of men. The light shines in darkness and the darkness has not understood it" (John 1:4-5). He describes John the Baptist as one who has come "to testify concerning that Light" (vs. 7). He proclaims Christ as the "true Light, which gives light to every man" (vs. 9).

One of the reasons God is called Light is because light always has a source. The great Olympic cauldrons produce light over the stadium and everyone knows it is coming from that source. Even so, Jesus Christ is the ultimate source of all the light which we have in the world. He is the creator of physical light. Every source of light available to the created world from the sun, to the stars, to fossil fuels, to solar, wind, ethanol and nuclear energy was all part of God's creative gift to mankind. We would live in a physically darkened world if it were not for Christ. Light did not evolve—it was created.

God, as the Light of the world, reminds us that for light to be valuable it has to be used, it has to be followed. It is not enough just to recognize the source of light, we have to walk in the path where the light shines. Imagine that a high school contains two large gymnasiums. One of the gymnasiums is ready for a basketball game. The halogen lights are on and the court is brilliantly lit, bright enough that even the referees will have no problem seeing what is going on. But as the teams come out of the locker rooms they don't run into that gymnasium. Instead they head into the other room which is still in the dark. All of those who have come to watch the game are sitting in the stands, in the dark. And they proceed to play the entire game in the dark. They know that the light is there. They believe that the light is there in the other room. But they choose to walk in darkness.

Even though they had access to the very Light of God, the religious leaders during the time of Christ chose to walk in darkness. Some did so out of loyalty to friends. Others made the choice because they saw upholding their own version of the law as their obligation. They thought they were doing what was right, but Jesus said their eyes were blinded.

DARE to "walk in the light as He is in the light" (I John 1:7). A world in darkness seeks to convince the believer that human progress and intelligence have eliminated any need for God. They argue against any system of absolutes. But God is still Light, and all that is apart from God is darkness. We either walk in Light or we walk in darkness. Even good character traits can lead us to walk in darkness when we fail to honor God. In your notebook take each of the following virtues and give an example of how they can be used for good or for evil, to keep us in the Light or to lead us into darkness.

Friendship.

Work.

Loyalty.

Compassion.

Perseverance.

Dare Twenty

God Omnipresent

"If I go up to the heavens, you are there; if I
make my bed in the depths, you are there.
If I rise on the wings of the dawn, if I settle
on the far side of the sea,
even there your hand will guide me, your right
hand will hold me fast."
Psalm 139:8-10

The population of Maxwell, Nebraska
includes less than 400 people. When one teenage girl
obtained her driver's license her mother shared with
her a loving warning. "No matter where you go in
town and what you do behind that wheel, I will know
about it before you get home." The writer of
Proverbs offered a similar message to his son when
he wrote, "The eyes of the Lord are everywhere,

keeping watch on the wicked and the good" (Proverbs 15:3).

The truth concerning God's presence in every place and at every time can become for us a caution against doing what is wicked or an incentive for doing what is good. But in either case it is the very fact of his omnipresence which makes the difference.

Omnipresence is clearly taught in scripture, but can also be inferred from the rest of God's attributes. Since He is Spirit, God has no dependence on the material world. He is not confined by matter and therefore has no boundaries on where He exists. Knowing that God is our Creator reminds us that He also created time and space. The Creator is greater than the creation, so time and space do not place limits on Him in any way. Psalm 139 describes in a very practical way how there is no place we can go but that God is already there.

God is in no way confined to the material world. He is present in every flower, but we cannot then say that the flower is God. Every avenue of scientific endeavor deserves study simply because it reveals the very nature of God. His omnipresence assures the steady constancy of what we call the laws of nature. The very fact that He is there holds all things together. At the same time, were all to pass away, He would still be there.

DARE to practice the presence of God. Read the following verses and list the practical applications which should become a part of the life of the believer as a result of understanding the attribute of omnipresence. Write your observations in your notebook.

Matthew 5:34-37 – Since God is present everywhere what should be our attitude toward truth-telling?

Matthew 6:9-10 – What impact should omnipresence have on the conduct of our prayer lives?

Acts 7:48-49 – Knowing that God is present everywhere should lead us to what truths concerning worship?

Acts 17:27-28 – Omnipresence should affect our daily conduct in what fashion?

Dare Twenty-One

God is Faithful

"If we are unfaithful, he remains faithful, for
he cannot deny who he is."
II Timothy 2:13 (NLT)

Old Shep still waits for his master in Fort
Benton, Montana. As the story goes, a sheep herder
needing medical attention boarded an east-bound train
to see a doctor. Watching him leave on that train was
his sheep dog, a dog named Shep. For the next five
and a half years Shep met every train coming into
Fort Benton waiting for his master to return. "Two
and a half years into the watch, Old Shep was
featured in *Ripley's Believe It Or Not*, and became a
Depression-era sensation." (RoadsideAmerica.com).
On January 12, 1942, the waiting came to an
end. Deaf and battling with arthritis, Shep slipped on

115

an icy rail and was hit by one of the trains he had run out to meet. Shep was buried by the entire town on a hill overlooking the train station. The Great Northern Railroad erected a painted cutout of his image with the words SHEP spelled out in white stones. Over the years the memorial has been maintained and upgraded so that Old Shep, the faithful dog, still waits for his master.

The faithfulness of God is in a real sense the outworking of His immutability. Since He never changes it naturally follows that He will always be faithful. Nothing will ever change the fact that He will forgive those who come to Him confessing their sin. God's faithfulness extends to all of His other attributes as well. His love will never change toward those who love Him. His justice will never change toward those who hate him (cf. Deuteronomy 7:9-10). God does not change His mind concerning the promise of eternal salvation. He will never fail to protect us from the attacks of Satan. No matter how many times we prove unfaithful to Him, He cannot be anything but faithful. It is part of His very nature.

The promise God made to Abraham concerning his heir was kept by a faithful God even when it seemed humanly impossible for Abraham and Sarah to have children. The prophetic promises made throughout Old Testament times were fulfilled by a faithful God in countless ways through the birth, life, death and resurrection of Christ. The promise to save all who will come to God through Jesus Christ has proved God faithful in every instance faith has been applied for thousands of years. The promise of a faithful God to restore the land of Israel to His chosen people provides current day evidence of His unchanging faithfulness. We can trust every promise from the Bible which has not yet been fulfilled as well because He is faithful.

The quality of faithfulness becomes one of the fruits of the Spirit which the indwelling of the Spirit seeks to produce in our lives as well (Galatians 5:22-23). Through the process of sanctification we are gradually being transformed into those who are like Christ, the Son of God. We will never be completely faithful as God is faithful, but we can move and grow in that direction. Like every other attribute of God which we are called to mirror, our faithfulness will at best be only a faint reflection of the faithfulness of God.

At some times in history a handshake sufficed as a pledge to faithfulness in even some of the most lucrative business deals. A man's word was his bond. DARE to become like God in faithfulness.

Prepare a document in your notebook indicating your resolve to be faithful. After each declarative statement sign your name, promising to allow the Holy Spirit to produce godly faithfulness in you as you are daily transformed into His image. Some areas of promise are listed below, but feel free to add those statements of promise which affect the way you live in this world.

I promise to remain faithful in every way to my marriage vows.

I promise to commit to faithfulness in my work for an employer.

I promise to do my best to be faithful in all assignments required by a teacher.

I promise to be faithful in raising my family in godly nurture.

I promise to be faithful to God in obedience to His Word.

Dare Twenty-Two

God is Good

"He loveth righteousness and judgment; the
earth is full of the goodness of the Lord."
Psalm 33:5 (KJV)

A gallery owner tells one of his artists that he
has some good news and some bad news. The artist
asks for the good news first. "Well," he replies, "the
good news is that a man came in here today asking if
the price of your paintings would go up after you
died. When I told him they would, he bought every
single one of your paintings." Elated, the artist asked,
"What could the bad news possibly be?"

"Evidently, that man was your doctor."
(sermon central.com).

Like Knock-Knock jokes, Good News, Bad News has evolved over the years into a joke genre of its own. As humans we have come to expect that even our good news will soon be balanced by something equally bad. In stark contrast to that pessimistic and realistic outlook on life stands the truth of God's goodness. With God there is never a good news-bad news situation. Everything God does is good.

At the end of creation week, before sin entered the world, God declared everything in the universe to be very good. Since God "cannot be tempted with evil" (James 1:13), He cannot be blamed for sin. Everything untouched by sin in the entire universe still fits that description of a very good work of God.

We find it easy to associate the goodness of God with His work of redemption. God loves those who are His enemies, plans and accomplishes salvation through Christ's sacrifice and welcomes into His family those who choose to receive adoption as sons. But those who remain His enemies still benefit from His goodness as well. "He causes his sun to rise on the evil and the good, and sends rain on the righteous and the unrighteous." (Matthew 5:45). The seasons of the year which bring growing seasons and harvests demonstrate His goodness. He is the giver of life, the source of all wisdom, and the provider of comfort in sorrow.

God's offer of salvation remains good whether or not people choose to accept that offer. His goodness does not increase when more people turn to Him and seek forgiveness nor does it diminish when multitudes reject Him. His goodness does not favor one ethnic group over another for He is "good to all" (Psalm 145:9). We must never think that His goodness intensifies in times of prosperity and shrinks in times of need. As long as we associate divine goodness with material prosperity we will arrive at incorrect conclusions. The goodness of God does not vary based upon our circumstances. He is good when we are rich and He is good when we are poor. God remains good whether we eat well or go hungry. His goodness does not depend on our satisfaction or distress. We do not determine the goodness of God. We accept His goodness and trust that whatever we face will accomplish His good purposes in our lives.

DARE to celebrate the goodness of God in your life. Contemplate this wonderful attribute and in your notebook start to compile a list of all the ways God has been good to you. Feel free to include the material while at the same time not overlooking the spiritual blessings our good God has given.

Dare Twenty-Three

God is Just

"The Lord reigns, let the earth be glad;
let the distant shores rejoice.
Clouds and thick darkness surround him;
righteousness and justice are the foundation of
his throne."
Psalm 97:1-2

Blind Justice, the commonly depicted image
of a blind-folded woman holding scales and a sword,
dates back many centuries. "The modern image of
Justice that many of us know today is based on
Greco-Roman mythology of Themis and Justitia.
Justitia, c. 1AD, is the Roman goddess of Justice and
was often portrayed as evenly balancing both scales
and a sword and often wearing a blindfold."
(itsaboutjustice.com). The scales represented the
balance between the interests of the parties involved

in the judicial decision. The sword spoke of the power of the law and the need for punishment of crime. The blindfold symbolized equality. A just decision required that the judge be unprejudiced, showing no favor for any of the parties involved.

Achieving justice in human courts has long been called in question by many inside and outside the legal system. Many judges have dedicated themselves to a lifetime of striving for the impartial decision-making expected by all those who end up in a courtroom. At the same time charges of political influence, ideological prejudice and outright bribery have been far too common.

The description of perfect justice from the One known as the Branch in Isaiah, sounds at first like He will also execute blind justice. "He will not judge by what he sees with his eyes, or decide by what he hears with his ears; but with righteousness he will judge the needy, with justice he will give decisions for the poor of the earth." (Isaiah 11:3-4). However, the justice of God cannot be termed blind. Instead it will not be necessary for Him to interrogate eye-witnesses or listen to oral testimony which may well be tainted. When God deals in justice He never makes a mistake because He already knows perfectly what has happened and who is guilty. He remains totally just because He is completely all-knowing.

When used of God the words justice and righteousness become interchangeable, something which is not true of human legal systems. A human law which violates divine law can be administered justly and still be unrighteous. A righteous decision according to the law of God may be termed unjust in the eyes of a society which ignores God. Only in the Person of God will we ever find justice and righteousness united perfectly.

The justice of God merges perfectly with His love and mercy. None of His attributes exist outside of His being, compelling Him to do something. God does not have to do something because Justice demands it. He condemns the sinner because He is just, even as he shows mercy to the repentant because He is love. Goodness without justice remains impossible. Perfect justice arises only from perfect holiness. A judge who sets aside the law as a personal favoritism toward the prisoner disqualifies himself from the bench. Justice demands punishment. Because the demands of the law were fully met through the sacrifice of Christ, God can be "just and the one who justifies those who have faith in Jesus" (Romans 3:26).

The existence of hell should remind us of the importance of the justice of God. Holiness cannot abide the presence of sin in any fashion and justice demands that sin be punished eternally. Seeing righteousness and justice in union shows us how the same God who prepares heaven for the righteous prepares hell for the unjust. Justice cannot permit sin in heaven any more than righteousness can condemn the justified to hell.

Since God alone is Just we do not bear the responsibility of legislating righteousness in the world around us. There will be times when our souls will be grieved by the evil in the world and the inadequacy of human government to eradicate wickedness. At the same time, we have been called to holiness and should strive to achieve the union of righteousness and justice in our own lives through the power of the indwelling Spirit.

DARE to become a righteous judge in regard to your own temptation to sin. From the following scriptural list of sins identify the one which poses the greatest temptation for you at the present time. Write out an accusation from the viewpoint of a prosecuting attorney who is seeking a just sentence against you before a judge. Describe that sin in language which you believe a holy God would use. Don't make excuses, but rather expose sin for the evil it really is in the sight of God.

Sexual immorality.

Impurity.

Debauchery.

Idolatry.

Witchcraft.

Hatred.

Discord.

Jealousy.

Fits of rage.

Selfish ambition.

Dissensions.

Factions.

Envy.

Drunkenness.

Orgies.

(List from Galatians 5:19-20)

Once we have become transparent concerning the wickedness which lies within our own hearts, we will begin to understand the magnitude of God's forgiveness, the purity of His justice and the immensity of His mercy. Once we have confessed sin and sought spiritual cleansing we can find consolation in His justice. Next to the judicial charges you have brought against yourself write those words from Romans 8:1, "there is now no condemnation for those who are in Christ Jesus."

Dare Twenty-Four

God is Merciful

"O give thanks unto the Lord, for He is good,
for His mercy endureth forever."
Psalm 136:1 (KJV)

Brad Bright in his series "Discover God" makes a necessary distinction between mercy and tolerance. "We have tried to reduce God to our size, to our standards, and to what we feel He ought to be like. This makes us feel comfortable. Too often we want Him to respond like we would respond to sin and injustice. We want Him to accept us on our standards of behavior." (discovergod.com). God does not tolerate sin, but rather He chooses to act in mercy toward the sinner. God is both just and merciful. He punishes sin and invites the sinner to come to Him in mercy.

Tolerance says that we must accept every action and every viewpoint as equally valid. Mercy recognizes the suffering and guilt and need brought upon the human race by its fall into sin and offers a lovingkindness totally undeserved by fallen man. Mercy does not overlook sin or condone sin or minimize sin. Instead God in His mercy demonstrates the very destructiveness of sin by giving to man a solution to sin completely unavailable to him through any effort or work of his own.

Mercy is compassion toward someone whom we have the power to punish. God describes Himself as a God of mercy when He met with Moses on top of Mt. Sinai (cf. Exodus 34:6-7). He offers His mercy freely while at the same time bringing justice upon those who continue to choose sinful ways. At the Red Sea He showed mercy to the children of Israel while bringing justice to the armies of Egypt. Both are essential qualities of His character.

The difference between God's mercy demonstrated toward all mankind and His special mercy enjoyed by the redeemed helps us understand this attribute as well. God's mercy toward all is seen in the preservation of the earth and its creatures. He provides food for animals who neither plant nor reap. He sends rain on both the just and the unjust. He prepared a world for us which is full of beauty and perfectly equipped to sustain life. He possesses the power to immediately punish sin, and yet He remains longsuffering, granting evil persons many years of life in which they have time to repent. None of His mercy is deserved. Food and shelter, life and beauty, comfort and health are not owed to the human race. The enmity of mankind against God deserves punishment. Those in rebellion against Him should have to depend on their own master, Satan. But Satan cannot give food and shelter. His wage for sin is death and the result of sin is ugliness instead of beauty. Sin leads to ruined health and hate instead of comfort.

Mercy must always be understood in conjunction with justice. God does not owe us mercy. We have earned condemnation, and mercy comes from the lovingkindness of God in ways we will never deserve.

God's special mercy comes upon those who, though deserving of punishment for sin, accept His gift of redemption. They realize that He has chosen them as objects of His mercy. He has provided a Savior who willingly went to the cross in order to obtain our redemption. He has forgiven our sin, placing it upon His Son, instead of requiring our just punishment. He has regenerated us, given us a new life in Christ, released us from bondage to Satan. He has granted us mercy in the coming day of judgment so that we will enjoy eternal life with Him according to His everlasting mercies.

DARE to celebrate the mercy of God. Examples of mercy which people offer to other people always pale in comparison to what God in His mercy has done for us. Acts of kindness are wonderful. Feeding the hungry and clothing the naked and building homes for the homeless exhibit compassion. But very few of us will ever be able to show compassion toward someone we have the right to punish, while at the same time remaining just in our conduct. Not one of us will ever be able to offer mercy to sinners based upon our own substitutionary sacrifice in taking their place and bearing their punishment. God's mercy remains without equal.

Consider once again the list of sins from Galatians 5:19-20.

Sexual immorality.

Impurity.

Debauchery.

Idolatry.

Witchcraft.

Hatred.

Discord.

Jealousy.

Fits of rage.

Selfish ambition.

Dissensions.

Factions.

Envy.

Drunkenness.

Orgies.

After each word describe the punishment which a person deserves for participation in each of those sins. Allow the overwhelming magnitude of the repulsive reality of sin to increase your appreciation and thankfulness for the overwhelming significance of the value of God's mercy in our lives.

Dare Twenty-Five

God is Love

"Whoever does not love does not know God,
because God is love."
I John 4:8

The runaway best-selling Harry Potter series has popularized the notion of magical protection provided by the power of love. Lord Voldemort finds it impossible to possess Harry completely because of the love Potter received from his parents and demonstrates toward others, something Voldemort knows nothing about. "If there is one thing Voldemort cannot understand it is love. He didn't realize that love as powerful as your mother's for you leaves its own mark. To have been loved so deeply, even though the person who loves us is gone, will give us some protection forever. It is in your very skin." (Rowling, "Harry Potter and the Sorcerer's Stone").

Love may be at once the most admired and least understood of all the attributes of God. God is love, but love is not God, and love is not all there is of God. Love is very real, but it is not magical. The love of God is bestowed universally upon on, but does not outweigh or limit any other attribute of God. God's love is holy, unchanging and just.

In order to apply biblical truth rather than human speculation to our understanding of the love of God, we must recognize that love existed long before the creation of the world. While it is true that God loves the world, love did not begin in the Garden of Eden nor is it limited to our relationship with Him. Love in eternity past characterized the Persons of the Trinity. The Father loves the Son and the Spirit. The Son loves the Father, and the Spirit also shares this attribute of love (cf. John 3:35, John 14:31, Galatians 5:22). This love was eternal, complete and perfect within the Godhead. The Father, Son and Spirit did not need us in order to show love. Had they needed something outside of themselves they would not have been perfect. Divine love is bestowed by choice and not because of an unfulfilled need.

Human love, by contrast, often originates in inward recognition of unfulfilled need. I need someone to love so that I will feel complete. I need someone to love so that I matter to someone. I need someone to love in order to feel like I have a purpose in life, someone depends on me. God's love always focuses on bringing about the best for the object of that love because He does not need anyone to complete him or make Him important or give Him a purpose in life.

God's love is not offered in response to our beauty or wisdom or love for Him. He loves the world when the world is unlovable, at enmity with Him. He offers love to those who He knows perfectly, with all their faults and failures. God loves even those who refuse His love. He loves in order to make men holy, not because they are holy. His love seeks constantly for our best rather than simply wanting to satisfy our desires. His love never changes no matter how we change toward Him. His love will never increase or diminish. He loves because we have a need for His love, not because He has a need for ours. So His love is totally genuine and honest, never duplicitous or manipulative.

God finds great joy in the objects of His love. He proclaimed the original creation "very good" (Genesis 1:31) because His love had provided the best for His creatures. His love is "higher than the heavens" (Psalm 108:4) reminding us that all of the universe carries the mark of His choice to do what is best for His material cosmos. Every star and sun and moon, every planet and asteroid has been placed with care into a sustained and smoothly functioning whole. The created universe is not in chaos, for "in Him all things hold together" (Colossians 1:17).

The love of God will never end. Our body and soul will be separated by death, but death cannot separate us from the love of God. Heaven and earth will pass away but God's love, which existed before creation, will continue on for all eternity. In this life we may suffer the loss of all things, but will never be without the love of God. Our minds may fall prey to the ravages of time and forget even those we love, but God will never forget His love for us. Friends may forsake us or betray us, but His love will never change.

Love is considered one of the transitive attributes which can in a very limited sense be shared by God's creatures. DARE to discover the love of God. Read once again Paul's excellent discourse on love in I Corinthians 13. As you read, think about the various descriptions of love, not in terms of our own experience, but in relationship to the love of God. In your notebook record each phrase in verses 4-8, applying them to God and reveling in what they teach us about His amazing love.

Example:

"Love is patient and kind." (I Cor. 13:4).

God will never grow tired of loving me. His love will cause Him to treat me with kindness no matter what circumstance I face in this life. He will never be anything but kind.

Dare Twenty-Six

God is Holy

"And they were calling to one another: "Holy, holy, holy is the LORD Almighty; the whole earth is full of his glory."
Isaiah 6:3

At the time of its discovery in 1901 the code of Hammurabi was understood to contain the earliest known written laws. Since that time other laws have been discovered including the Ur-Nammu law code which pre-dates Hammurabi by three hundred years. "Then did Ur-Nammu the mighty warrior, king of Ur, king of Sumer and Akkad, by the might of Nanna, lord of the city, and in accordance with the true word of Utu, establish equity in the land; he banished malediction, violence and strife." (historyofinformation.com).

The existence of ancient law codes does not surprise us in the present age. Violence, strife, lying, stealing, and dishonesty permeate the history of man. The natural reaction of civilization has been to protect itself through a system of legal rules enforced by those entrusted with the maintenance of harmony in human government. Even in the instance of a corrupt government it is generally conceded that enforcement of some law is better than total anarchy.

When we consider the holiness of God we must first remind ourselves that God is not holy because of conformity to some outward standard of holiness. Holiness exists because God Himself is holy. He sets the standard of holiness. If God had to conform to some other standard, those rules would be greater than God. They would require Him to change and we have already learned that God cannot change. So holiness must be understood as the righteousness which God possesses, and unholiness is then anything which does not conform to His perfect standard. Morality does not depend on community standards or cultural preferences or evolving opinions.

God's holiness is seen through His actions. He created a world which was totally good and a race of humans morally innocent. His reaction to the entrance of sin into the world involved righteous judgment and a punishment designed to bring about correction so that man could once again be holy. The sacrifices offered as a covering for sin throughout the years of life under the Law had to be holy sacrifices to satisfy a holy God. They needed to be offered with a pure heart or they were not acceptable. When Christ came in the flesh and lived as a man, He remained untainted by sin, living a human life which was completely holy. In that way He could provide a perfect sacrifice which removed sin rather than simply covering it over as the Old Testament sacrifices had done.

God's perfect love is seen in His desire to impart holiness to mankind. Love desires the best for the one loved, and moral purity or holiness is the very best for the human race. God's holiness does not deny joy and pleasure and satisfaction to us. Instead it assures us the greatest joy, the ultimate pleasure and the supreme satisfaction. Our supreme satisfaction comes from reconciliation and fellowship with God. Sin has its first and greatest effect upon our relationship with God rather than our relationship with self or with others. It separates us from God because God is perfect in holiness.

Satan may offer "the fleeting pleasures of sin" (Hebrews 11:25), but only God's holiness brings complete satisfaction to the heart and soul. To separate God's love from God's holiness results in a conflict which does not exist. God will never allow because of love what He does not require on account of holiness. He loves us in our sin for the purpose of redeeming us from sin and making us holy. God is first of all holy and then desires holiness in us. That will never change. He will never regard the immoral as moral or the impure as pure. Holiness remains part of His nature and therefore every action of God will be holy.

For our love to be like God's, it must also desire holiness for the one loved.   Godly love will never become an excuse for unholiness. To argue that a sinful action must be right because two people love each other is to totally twist divine love into something false and evil.

DARE to accept God's challenge to "Be holy, because I am holy" (I Peter 1:16). That will happen only as the imparted holiness of Christ gains control over our actions through the process of sanctification. Holiness movements have historically emphasized the passivity of a holy lifestyle. Words they often use to describe holiness have included meditation, prayer, fasting and solitude. Some have even concluded that true holiness demands a total physical separation from the world. The holiness of God appears not only in the Being of God but in His Willing. He is active in holiness and expects us to be holy in daily life as well as in solitude. Read the following verses which describe the holiness of God in action. In your notebook record specific ways in which we can be like God in holiness while living and working in this present world.

Example: Psalm 47:8

God's action: He rules and reigns in holiness.

Our action: We must be totally just and righteous in any position of authority and power which we may occupy.

Isaiah 6:3

God's action:

Our action:

Isaiah 57:15

God's action:

Our action:

I Corinthians 3:17

God's action:

Our action:

Hebrews 7:26

God's action:

Our action:

Dare Twenty-Seven

God is Sovereign

"Which God will bring about in His own
time—He who is blessed and the only
Sovereign One, the King of kings
and Lord of lords."
I Timothy 6:15

According to the Spanish constitution of 1978 the official title of their ruler is King of Spain. But the historical titles held by that king are also listed including such designations as King of Leon, King of Aragon, King of the West and East Indies and King of Jerusalem. The kingdom of Jerusalem was lost in 1191 but the title was still invested to King Don Carlos as late as 1738. The King of Spain also carries the title of Archduke of Austria on account of the marriage of Juana with archduke Philip of Austria in

1496. Thirty-seven honorifics for the king are listed including Sovereign Grand-Master of the Order of the Golden Fleece. That title has been contested with the Austrian Hapsburgs since 1700 with both houses continuing to award the order separately (see heraldica.org).

Titles related to sovereignty date back hundreds of years, but very few rulers have held those titles for any great length of time. Teodoro Obiang Nguema Mbasogo has been in power in Equatorial Guinea since 1979 (cnbc.com). The present Queen of England has been on the throne since 1953. Most reigns are much briefer.

The sovereignty of God simply means that He rules over all. God alone decided how He would create the worlds. His will and word formed the cosmos without advice from any othe, for there was no other but Him. He had the power and authority to make every atom, every element, every design exactly as He pleased. His creative hand was not compelled by anything else but His sovereign will and pleasure.

God remains sovereign over all His creation. What we often call providence is simply the outworking of His sovereign will. Birth and death alike are in His hands. Where a person is raised, the circumstances of their condition in life, the honor they receive or the poverty they endure, sickness and health are all alike under the control of His sovereignty. Such a truth does not negate a person's efforts to better self, to care for the health of the body and to move to a better location should he so choose. Matters of industry and education and advancement in medical science are likewise part of the sovereign plan of God. In His sovereignty is included the free will He has given to the human race.

All governments remain subject to the sovereign rule of God. We may not understand how He can allow evil men to rule over others but we have been told that "the Most High is sovereign over all kingdoms on earth and gives them to anyone he wishes and sets over them the lowliest of people." (Daniel 4:17). Why He sometimes chooses the lowliest to rule has not been revealed, but we can find assurance in the fact that God knows what He is doing and doesn't need our advice.

The fact that God rules over all certainly includes the spiritual realm as well as the political and material realms. One of the chief questions asked when sovereignty is in view concerns the origin of sin. The holiness of God posits a Being completely pure and untainted by evil in any way. He will never tempt anyone to sin and is in no way responsible for the sinful acts of either the fallen angels or fallen man. While we may never in this life completely understand why God has permitted evil, we can know that God's plan for the human race included endowing them with a free will. The choice to use that will in order to sin remains the responsibility of the angels and the human race which chose to sin. "Man's will is free because God is sovereign. A God less than sovereign could not bestow moral freedom upon His creatures. He would be afraid to do so." (Tozer).

The gifts of God's grace are also given according to His sovereign will. These gifts are given to the church, the body of Christ, in order that we might accomplish the tasks entrusted to us. There is no need to covet the gift someone else has received. What we have been given should be used to the very best of our ability in service to Him.

Accepting the fact that God remains sovereign in our lives may be one of the most difficult assignments God gives to His own. Even as believers our tendency is to desire to reign in our own lives. We want to make our own decisions, to solve our own problems and to revenge our own wrongs.

DARE to walk on the water of the sovereignty of God.

Physically go through the act of turning control of your entire life over to God. Find a private place and designate a chair or bench as the throne of your life. Construct a paper crown to place on your head and take a seat on that chair. It is important to perform this worship scenario in a way which is only between you and God. While sitting on the chair open your heart to God and acknowledge His sovereign power over your life. Accept the way He has made you, the gifts He has given and the salvation you have received. Confess your inner desire to take control away from Him and seek His forgiveness for your rebellion. As you are praying, get up from the chair, place the crown where you were seated and prostrate yourself before a holy God. Invite Him to take complete control. Ask for His own strength to help you yield daily to the wisdom and guidance of His will. You don't need to leave the chair there or make it into some kind of shrine because God will be on the throne everywhere you go. Determine to continually seek the rule and reign of God in your life, never again trying to replace Him on His throne.

Dare Twenty-Eight

God Is Truth

"Jesus answered, "I am the way and the truth
and the life. No one comes to the Father
except through me."
John 14:6

Two men had an argument. To settle the
matter, they went to a Sufi judge for arbitration. The
plaintiff made his case. He was very eloquent and
persuasive in his reasoning. When he finished, the
judge nodded in approval and said, "That's right,
that's right."

On hearing this the defendant jumped up and
said, "Wait a second, judge, you haven't even heard
my side of the case yet." So the judge told the
defendant to state his case. And he, too, was very

persuasive and eloquent. When he finished, the judge said, "That's right, that's right."

When the clerk of the court heard this, he jumped up and said, "Judge, they both can't be right." The judge looked at the clerk of court and said, "That's right, that's right." (von Oech, "A Whack on the Side of the Head").

Truth, the real facts about anything, remains one of the most elusive of qualities in regard to humanity. One of the reasons for that elusiveness lies in the influence of the one who is the father of lies. "When he lies, he speaks his native language, for he is a liar and the father of lies." (John 8:44).

The contrast between the Devil and God is exemplified in every part of their being, but perhaps is no more evident than in the matter of truth and falsehood. God is truth in everything He says and does. The Devil is a deceiver in everything he says and does.

God is the source of all truth. All truth whether logical, mathematical, scientific or religious has its foundation in the God of truth. As a result, that which is true reveals facts about God. Every society maintains standards of right and wrong, acknowledging that good and evil exist in the world. That fact reveals the holiness of God as well as the truth that He has placed a conscience into the heart of every individual. Those who deny the existence of God go to great lengths to remove Him from the truth of any subject they study.

God is true in what He says. He cannot lie (cf. Numbers 23:19). Every lie ever told patterns itself after Satan, who does nothing but lie, and not after God. Truth cannot be changed because God never changes. So, truth is not relative, but absolute. Logical puzzles have long existed in an attempt to disprove the existence of absolute truth. A person might say, "As soon as I voice the fact that there are 318.9 million people in the United States some people will have died and others will have been born so I did not really tell the truth." That potential dilemma does not prove that truth does not exist. There is a specific population in the U.S.A. at any given point in time. It only proves that I do not have the mental capability of knowing that particular fact. God not only knows the exact number, He even knows how many hairs each of those people have on their heads (cf. Luke 12:7).

God is also true in all His works. The reason God offers mercy lies in the fact that He knows the truth about us. He knows that we need mercy and is not surprised by the evil which lies in the hearts of men. We will never deceive Him, even if we lie to ourselves and convince ourselves that we are good. He knows the truth about us and we should never cheapen His mercy by denying the truth concerning our own hearts. God's justice is also based on the fact that He is the truth. His judgment promises are just as true as His blessing promises. The entire history of Israel has been recorded for us in order to remind us of that fact. No one will ever be able to stand before God and claim a mistrial. He knows what we have don,e and he knows what is in our hearts. He can know nothing else, because He is Truth.

DARE to trust the God of Truth.

This series, "Dare To Walk On Water" includes a workbook which introduces a believer to a personal method of Bible study. This workbook provides a way in which you can understand, interpret and apply the truth of the Word of God to your own life. Like this devotional and the others in the series, it does not stop with understanding the Word or even trusting the Word. It moves beyond to specific creative actions we can do because of what we know, feel and believe. Since God is truth, His Word is truth. Obtain your copy of "Dare To Walk On Water: The Workbook" and start on the marvelous adventure of seeing your life transformed by conforming your mind and actions to the truth of God's Word.

Dare Twenty-Nine

God Almighty

"Then I heard what sounded like a great
multitude, like the roar of rushing waters and
like loud peals of thunder, shouting:
"Hallelujah!
For our Lord God Almighty reigns."
Revelation 19:6

The immensely popular Star Wars franchise
brought into contemporary literature the concept of a
"Force" or energy field that connects everything in
the universe and could be tapped into by those
sensitive to its existence. Obi-Wan Kenobi described
it in this fashion to Luke Skywalker. "Well, the Force
is what gives a Jedi his power. It's an energy field
created by all living things. It surrounds us and
penetrates us; it binds the galaxy together" (Star
Wars: Episode IV).

A similar power has been part of Hindu thought for many centuries. Although there are differences, the description of "Brahman" sounds very similar to that of the "Force." "There is a power which pervades the cosmos, linking everything there is, and by tapping into it human beings can come into communication with the divine." (Burke, "The Major Religions").

One characteristic shared by both of these entities reminds us of the vital difference between such ideas and the omnipotence of God. The Force and the Brahman are both impersonal. The All-power which is one of the attributes of Almighty God is part of a wise, loving, holy and gracious Person. The modern mind feels far more comfortable with an impersonal law of nature or scientific hypothesis than with a Personal God.

The omnipotence of God is also unchanging, eternal and loving. Using energy, as in the creation of the world, does not diminish the energy of God in any fashion. He does not need to replenish the power He exerts. Human means of renewing physical energy like eating, sleeping, relaxing, exercising and vacationing are unnecessary to God. His might never varies and never needs to be restored.

The same power God used when He founded the universe and the same power exerted when He raised Christ from the dead belong to God today. No power will ever rise to challenge Him. We must never think of God in a defensive mode, isolated on His throne and under attack by forces He cannot control. He never exceeds His limits because He has no limits. There will never be a time when He does not have the strength to help us because that strength is eternal and infinite.

We can trust in and rejoice in the omnipotence of God because the God who is All-powerful is also All-loving. Dictatorships, with one person in control of all legal, political, financial and military systems of a country have proved to be a very efficient means of government. At the same time, they have been disastrous for the populace because of the greed, prejudice, hatred and self-serving of human leaders. God's wisdom, love and justice make Him the perfect Sovereign. His might includes the ability to accomplish what His wisdom ordains. His power is never misused because of His love. His justice combined with omnipotence causes Him to rule in absolute righteousness so that the wicked and not the innocent are punished, and all are offered His grace.

The third Person of the Trinity, the Holy Spirit, is often described in scripture in terms which illustrate His might. Wind, water and fire are all used as similes of His power. The force of wind finds its greatest effect in hurricane or tornadic activity. But prevailing winds circulate air over the entire planet, bring the rain clouds and initiate cool breezes. Both the beneficial and destructive powers of wind are only material examples of the power possessed by God the Holy Spirit. Moving water has the ability to completely change the appearance of the landscape but its power is also seen in the fact that life cannot exist without water. Both heat and light come from the power of fire. Under control, the forces of wind, water and fire provide the basic comforts of life to all the world. Omnipotence in the hands of an impersonal Force should be feared. But the fact that a Personal God possesses omnipotence brings comfort to our souls.

DARE to yield control to the power of the Omnipotent God.

Take an afternoon off and fly kites with your children or grandchildren or a friend. As you watch the kite soar consider the power of the wind as an illustration of the omnipotence of the Holy Spirit. With the wind the kite can fly, without the wind it is powerless. You can find the place the wind is working and allow it to carry your kite aloft, but you cannot make the wind go where you want it to go. Your string and the control you maintain over the kite affects your kite, but it does not place any limit on the movement or the power of the wind.

Dare Thirty

God is Grace

"In him we have redemption through his
blood, the forgiveness of sins, in accordance
with the riches of God's grace"
Ephesians 1:7

Victor Hugo's classic "Les Miserables"
includes the fascinating account often excerpted and
simply called "The Bishop's Candlesticks." Jean
ValJean spent nineteen years in jail for stealing a loaf
of bread. Finally released, he walked through town
looking for work, eventually ending up at the door of
the Bishop of Digne. In spite of ValJean's past the
bishop invites him in, feeds him and offers him a
warm bed for the night. After everyone falls asleep,
Jean steals the bishop's silver plates and leaves the
house.

The next day the police show up at the bishop's door with Jean and the silver plate. To the amazement of everyone, including Jean, the bishop explains that he had given the silver to Jean and adds to what the man has stolen two silver candlesticks which he says Jean overlooked. When the police leave, the bishop tells Jean to take the silver and use the money to become an honest man (Hugo).

The difference between mercy and grace shines brightly through the imagery of that story. Mercy is demonstrated by the fact that the bishop does not prosecute Jean for what he had obviously done wrong. Grace is seen in the gift of the silver candlesticks which the bishop offers to a man who certainly does not deserve what he is being given.

Several words are used in the Old Testament and translated into grace in our English versions. The result is that grace and mercy can almost be used interchangeably. But grace usually refers to some favor which has been given without any conditions or stipulations. When Noah found grace in the eyes of the Lord (Genesis 6:8) it was not based on anything Noah had previously done. God acted in grace toward him even before the scripture calls him righteous and blameless and tells us that he walked with God. Those were results of God's grace and not the cause of His grace. God gave to Noah what he did not deserve.

We will never truly understand the awesome impact of grace until we come to the place where we see ourselves as completely unworthy and deserving nothing. Instead, most people in the modern world have a pretty high opinion of themselves. We think we are good people and conclude that God thinks the same of us. Until we see our sinfulness and spiritual degradation we will not understand the need for grace.

We will never truly understand the grace of God until we grasp the truth of the justice of God. Sin must be punished because God is holy, and sin will be punished because He is just. We excuse our own sins, tolerate the sins of others and assume that God is just like us. We think that punishment will never come, so what need is there for grace?

We will never appreciate the importance of the grace of God until we admit that we cannot please God. Nothing we can do will ever satisfy His righteous anger. We think that somehow our good works will outweigh our bad works or that He is too loving to punish sin. But when we think that, we do not know God. He would not be righteous if He simply allowed us to sin without punishment. We cannot earn His favor in any way, so we need grace.

We will never truly know the grace of God until we see it as a free gift, offered completely without compulsion of any kind. God does not need anything from us. He does not depend on our worship or our personal sacrifice. He does not owe us anything. We have by our sin earned for ourselves the wage of sin, which is death. Our only right is the right to receive condemnation. The fact that God has chosen to offer salvation, to free us from condemnation, comes totally from His grace.

DARE to grow in your appreciation for the grace of God. The book of Philemon demonstrates in a very practical way the manifestation of grace in a believer's life as a result of God's grace. The story concerns Paul, his friend Philemon and slave named Onesimus. Read the book, and in your notebook record your own impressions of what it means to know the grace of God, to live by that grace and to demonstrate grace toward others. Consider your own acquaintances and seek to discover an "Onesimus" of your own. Determine to dedicate yourself to seeking reconciliation between your "Onesimus" and your friend from whom he or she has become estranged. Allow the effort of that quest to open your eyes to the magnificence of the grace of God who seeks to reconcile all mankind to Himself.

Dare Thirty-One

God is Awake

"Indeed, he who watches over Israel will
neither slumber nor sleep."
Psalm 121:4

Insomnia can kill. An extremely rare genetic
disease, called fatal familial insomnia, turns sleeping
difficulty into total sleeplessness. A person who
cannot sleep deteriorates rapidly with physical and
mental stress, a condition which can cause death in
less than a year.

Sonia Vallabh watched her mother die at age
52 from FFI. "She couldn't walk or talk or feed
herself. She became deeply paranoid and fell into a
profound dementia. She went on life support, and
died a few weeks later." (Swartz, "Insomnia That
Kills"). Sonia harbors the gene and along with her

husband, Eric Minikel, has dedicated her life to studying this strange disease. They are looking for a cure.

The God who designed the human body knew the importance of sleep for those He created. Even those without this terrible disease become irritable and function at less than their best from a lack of sleep.

Isn't it interesting that the God who never sleeps provided the human race with exactly what we need to function effectively in the bodies He created? The absence of any need to sleep or rest or be refreshed in any way marks another of the tremendous ways in which God is different from the created world. That fact that He remains constantly awake and alert underlines the perfection of many of His other attributes as well.

The omnipotence of God always remains at full power because God never grows tired or takes a nap. When the prophet Elijah went into conflict with the prophets of Baal he mocked their god with the taunt, "maybe he is sleeping so that you will have to wake him," (I Kings 18:27). We will never need to worry about a time when God is powerless to help because He never sleeps.

When we sleep our awareness of the world around us diminishes to the place where we have no idea what is happening. That will never be the case with the wisdom of God. The promise to Israel in Psalm 121:4 came in the context of the need for help. The One who helps us in every area of life will always be available because He watches over us without sleeping.

The fact that God is Spirit drives home this truth with even greater force. He does not have eyes to close. He does not possess a body of muscles and tendons that grow tired from hard work. His mind is not composed of grey matter and synapses which weaken with age. There is nothing material about God that wears out and ages. He is from age to age the same.

DARE to depend on a God who never sleeps.

Above the light switch in your bedroom or hanging from the bedside lamp which you extinguish last before sleeping, post a note which reads: God is Awake! Reminding ourselves of that wonderful truth should help us relax and enjoy the good gift of sleep which God has graciously given us and which we so desperately need.

Dare Thirty-Two

God is Gentle

"The fruit of the Spirit is...gentleness."
Galatians 5:23

In the Wild West breaking horses meant climbing on the back of a stallion and staying there until the horse learned who was boss. This usually involved a period of bucking, jumping, running and other attempts to unseat the rider. Another method of training a wild horse to accept a saddle and human rider became known as horse whispering. A horse whisperer attempted to develop rapport with the horse by "gentle methods and speech" (dictionary.com). Although known since the 1800s, the method became popular through the 1995 Nicholas Evans book "The

Horse Whisperer," later turned into a movie by the same name.

Since gentleness is included as one of the fruits of the Spirit in Galatians 5:23 and the Spirit is the third Person of the God-head, gentleness can be identified as one of the characteristics of God. Gentleness involves treating others with mildness or sweet reasonableness. It is the opposite of harshness or severity.

The gentleness of God becomes evident when we consider the patience with which God treats a sinful world. Paul says that it is the kindness of God that "leads you toward repentance" (Romans 2:4). God has the perfect right to punish sin immediately in complete justice. When judgment upon sin comes it will be in accordance with His holy nature to punish the wicked. But sin does not face immediate judgment. The gentleness of God instead grants to the sinner time, time to consider what has been done, and time to respond to the love of the God who can free them from their bondage to sin.

God displays gentleness in the area of divine wisdom as well. He knows everything. He is truth. He knows what is best for us, and yet He is willing to teach us and to reason with us. In the words of the prophet Isaiah he says, "Come now and let us reason together," (Isa. 1:18). God could have simply revealed the Ten Commandments and the plan of salvation but He has given us 66 inspired books because He wants us to think. He wants us to know why. He desires to teach us and instruct us in the way we should go. He doesn't expect immediate maturity on the part of believers, but is gentle in His approach to the way we learn.

We can also see the gentleness of God in the fact that He works with each one of us individually, starting with the place where He finds us. He never demands that we achieve spiritual greatness on our own so that He can be proud of us. He instead gives us the Holy Spirit who generates spiritual life within us, progressively sanctifying us so that what we are becoming will be to the praise of His glory. Gentleness is God's grace in action. God is at work bringing help to those who do not deserve help.

The gentleness of God can be clearly seen in Jesus Christ, the personification of a quiet and gentle spirit. Though by right He was the King, He became a servant. Though all of the universe should have served Him, He chose to serve others. Christ deserved the highest honor, but He willingly chose to die that we might be restored to fellowship with God. Isaiah described Him long before He ever came to earth. "A bruised reed he will not break, and a smoldering wick he will not snuff out. In faithfulness he will bring forth justice." (Isaiah 42:3).

DARE to respond to the gentleness of God. Take a walk on a windy day and feel the breeze touching every part of your being. Think of the contrast between that breeze and the forceful winds of a tornado or hurricane. How much better it is to let a gentle wind guide you than to wait for the gale-force winds of a storm. Determine to follow the gentle leading of the Holy Spirit moving through your heart and life rather than waiting to be driven to obedience by the power of God's judgment.

Dare Thirty-Three

God is Longsuffering

"But the fruit of the Spirit is...longsuffering"
Galatians 5:22 (KJV)

Patience and Longsuffering can often be interchanged, considered as synonyms. However, one way of looking at them helps bring additional understanding. In many cases patience relates to showing courage under pressure from events and the trials we face in the world around us. Longsuffering shows the same steadfastness under pressure, but it usually relates to people. We demonstrate longsuffering when we endure ill-treatment from others without anger and thoughts of revenge.

Patience helps you deal with a car that won't start.

179

Longsuffering helps you deal with a son who is learning to drive and has flooded the engine.

Patience keeps you calm when the red light seems endless and there is no traffic.

Longsuffering keeps you calm when a flagman stops you and you can't see any reason for the delay.

Patience rules when your checking account won't balance.

Longsuffering rules when the collection agency calls about a bill you know you have already paid.

Patience teaches you to try again when the basketball won't go through the hoop.

Longsuffering teaches you to put up with the opponent who fouls you every time you try to shoot for the hoop and the referee who fails to notice.

God is patient. But He is also longsuffering. During the years leading up to the flood the neighbors of Noah maligned God by making fun of the preacher of righteousness. They misused the intelligence God had Himself given to them, and they mistreated God by ignoring the distinctions between the righteous and the unrighteous. God's reaction was one of longsuffering. He granted them one hundred and twenty years of warning before sending judgment.

When God the Son lived on earth, people refused to give Him the glory He deserved. They mocked him and accused Him of having a devil. They twisted His words and tried to convince people of the truth of things He never said. They cursed Him, beat Him and finally crucified Him even though He was innocent of any crime. Christ's reaction was to willingly go to the cross to redeem for all eternity those who had done their worst to Him.

The Apostle Paul describes the attitude of the world toward God in the first chapter of his epistle to the Romans. He says that men refuse to glorify Him. They refuse to thank Him for His goodness. They corrupt the thought of Him by making idols His equal. They turn His truth into a lie. They refuse to acknowledge that He even exists. They demonstrate their hatred of Him. They take pleasure in others who have their same attitude toward God. They despise all that He has done for them. What is God's attitude toward such people? Longsuffering. He reminds those very people who do those things that they are despising "the riches of his goodness and forbearance and longsuffering; not knowing that the goodness of God leadeth thee to repentance" (Romans 2:4 KJV).

DARE to respond to the longsuffering of God in your own life by learning to be like Him in your longsuffering with others.

Consider the following potential life situations and write in your notebook how a longsuffering God deals with each one of them. Then ask yourself how God wants you to develop longsuffering in your own life.

1. Someone close to you refuses to listen to the gospel. They remain your friend, but you really want to see them saved, yet because of their antagonism you have just about decided that you will never mention Jesus or salvation to them again unless they bring up the subject.

2. Your neighbor insists on telling anyone who will listen that you cheated him out of a foot of property when you put up your fence. You hired a surveyor to mark the border line before you even started and you know what he says is not true. But you really want to prove to everyone that he is a liar.

3. A teen-age child has rebelled and refuses to keep the curfew you as parents have established. You are

afraid of the influence this child has on your other children and are seriously considering refusing to allow her to live at home any longer.

Dare Thirty-Four

God is Peace

"But the fruit of the Spirit is...peace."
Galatians 5:22

According to the New York Times there have been only 268 years of peace in the world out of its entire history. In order to come to that statistic, war was defined as "an active conflict that has claimed more than 1,000 lives" (Hedges, "What Every Person Should Know About War"). The article used the figure of 3,400 years of recorded history to arrive at the estimate of how many years the world has been at peace.

Peace, as one of the fruits of the Spirit, describes what God the Holy Spirit as well as the Triune God must be like. Peace is often seen as the absence of war, but in reality peace comes with the conclusion of war. A state of peace means that one side has surrendered and another side has triumphed. As long as the triumphant side remains in power the world continues to live in peace.

Since God possesses the attribute of power, being the All-Mighty, He is really the only one who can maintain peace. The 1000-year millennial reign of Christ will be a time of peace because He will be Lord of lords and King of kings, ruling with a rod of iron (cf. Rev. 2:27). Recognizing God as a God of peace fits with every other attribute including omnipotence, majesty, power and sovereignty.

Too often those who desire a religion of peace believe that the road to peace is the road of tolerance toward wrong and surrender to sin. They teach a peace that comes from subjection and submission to the ways of the world rather than victory through Christ. That is not the peace that Jesus gives.

Peace with God comes from surrender, but not to sin. What we must do is surrender our will to His. The surrender begins at the cross where we leave the kingdom of darkness and submit ourselves to Him as members of the kingdom of the Son of God. Our sinful will becomes subject to His righteousness. Our choice to live in sin yields to His call to live in righteousness. We are no longer part of the kingdom of this world as slaves to sin but have become "free from your slavery to sin, and you have become slaves to righteous living." (Romans 6:18).

God is a God of peace because no weapon formed against Him can ever succeed. He will never be overthrown. In fact, there is really no force in the world which can even be a threat to Him. He does not sit on His throne in heaven battling fiercely against the powers of the wicked one trying to keep Satan from defeating Him. When the forces of the anti-Christ do come face to face with the power of God all it takes is a breath of air and a bright light to defeat him. "And then the lawless one will be revealed, whom the Lord Jesus will overthrow with the breath of his mouth and destroy by the splendor of his coming." (II Thessalonians 2:8).

One of the great titles accorded in scripture to the Son of God is Prince of Peace (cf. Isaiah 9:6). There are several lessons which can be learned concerning God from this characteristic of peace. A God at peace means that there is no dissension among the Persons of the Trinity. They do not disagree or argue or fight. There is not an Old Testament God who grows angry and a New Testament God who loves. God the Father, God the Son and God the Holy Spirit all possess and always will possess peace.

The fact that God is peace shows us that He will never be defeated. His promise of peace for all eternity to those who believe in Christ will certainly come to pass because nothing can disturb the peace of God. Every enemy will be destroyed and "every knee will bow before me; every tongue will acknowledge God" (Romans 14:11). So peace is the key to trust as well. We can trust Him to keep every promise because He is the Prince of Peace.

DARE to accept the truth that peace comes through submission to the will of God. Because of the sinful nature dominating humanity, God has also placed into each life those to whom we must submit in order to live at peace in this world. In your notebook, record the authority God has ordained in each of the following areas of life so that men and women may live in peace. In each case consider the impact of the difference between forced submission to authority and willing submission to authority.

Peace in the inner man – Authority – forced or willing?

Peace in the family – Authority – forced or willing?

Peace in the community – Authority – forced or willing?

Peace in the church – Authority – forced or willing?

Peace in the nation – Authority –forced or willing?

Peace between nations – Authority – forced or willing?

Dare Thirty-Five

God is Self-Controlled

"But the fruit of the Spirit is...self-control"
Galatians 5:22-23

"At the end of the nineteenth century Americans spent over a billion dollars on alcoholic beverages each year, compared with $900 million on meat, and less than $200 million on public education." (wctu.org). Because of the dangers of alcohol, the Women's Christian Temperance Union was formed in 1874. They desired through education and example, later supported by political activity, to convince people to abstain completely from alcohol, tobacco and other drugs. "In three months the women had driven liquor out of 250 communities, and for the first time felt what could be accomplished by standing together." (wctu.org).

The Women's Christian Temperance Union still exists today, and in addition to the fight against alcohol they have supported such causes as uniform marriage and divorce laws, founding of kindergartens, shelters for abused women and children, suffrage and the promotion of nutrition. One result of their activity has been the almost complete association of the word temperance with abstinence from drinking alcohol.

When the word temperance occurs in the fruit of the Spirit, as it does in the King James Version, the first reaction of most people causes them to think of the definition used by the WCTU. Certainly God, who is Spirit and does not depend on any food or drink to sustain life, does not imbibe alcoholic beverages. But the word must not be confined to that definition if we are to understand all that God has revealed about Himself. Ephesians 5:23 in other versions, including the NIV quoted at the beginning of this Dare, uses the word self-control. The connection between the two words becomes apparent when we realize that an intemperate person in regard to alcohol is not in control of himself. Alcohol has taken control of his mind and body.

God is always and completely in control of his own thoughts and actions. He is perfect in His self-control. That means that no other substance, influence or being outside of Himself ever changes the way He thinks or acts. When we think of self-control as a fruit the Spirit produces in our lives, we realize that it is not a license to do whatever we want to do because we are in control of our own bodies. Instead it is a self-control made possible by the indwelling of the Holy Spirit who enables us to remain under the control of the new creation we have been made in Christ Jesus. Sin and the power of sin no longer controls us. Instead we live a righteous, self-controlled life because Christ lives within.

The divine illustration of perfect self-control comes once again from the life of Christ. Every possible influence to sin put pressure upon Him while He lived as a man during the incarnation. He was "tempted in every way, just as we are—yet he did not sin." (Hebrews 4:15). Nothing from the outside ever held a greater sway over Him than His own inner character. During the time of His direct temptation from Satan he was not persuaded by offers of physical sustenance in spite of hunger. He did not fall prey to the temptation to require God to prove His care through miraculous protection. He refused to consider the offer of a sinful path to power and wealth (cf. Matthew 4:1-11). Not once in all the time He spent as a man did He lose control over His own thoughts, motives, emotions or actions.

DARE to impress on yourself in a visual fashion the importance of living under the control of the Holy Spirit. Assemble a group of bottles or cans and label them with all of the things which seek to control our lives apart from the Holy Spirit. These could include alcohol, drugs, peer pressure, guilt, jealousy, envy, pride, false doctrine, covetousness, desire for fame, money, nicotine, pornography, gluttony and any other lusts and desires to which men are prone. Set the labeled bottles or cans on the top of a fence and engage in target practice. Use a rifle or pistol, or if you don't have access to firearms use a slingshot or simply throw rocks. Each time you hit a target make a promise to God that you will yield to the power of the self-controlled Holy Spirit rather than allowing outside forces to control your mind and heart.

Dare Thirty-Six

God is Meek

"But the fruit of the Spirit is...meekness."
Galatians 5:22-23 (KJV)

Cartoonist Harold Tucker Webster created a
panel series called "The Timid Soul," originally
published in the New York World during the 1920s.
His most famous character Caspar Milquetoast
emerged as part of that series. Webster described
Milquetoast as "the man who speaks softly and gets
hit with a big stick." "A sign reading, 'Watch This
Space,' could render him motionless for hours."
(toonopedia.com).

The very name of this cartoon character has
come into our language as a synonym of meekness.
Milquetoast was spineless, subservient and lacking
any initiative or spirit. Knowing only that meaning of

the word meek, it would seem strange indeed to use it as a description of God. But meekness remains embedded in the list of the fruit of the Spirit which He wants to produce in our lives as well.

Like so many other English words, meek has lost much of its original meaning through contemporary usage. When used in scripture, and particularly when used of God, the word meek describes a person who is firm while at the same time gentle, decisive but fair in consideration of others. A meek person never loses his temper, but knows the right time to become passionate and even angry when evil must be dealt with severely.

Since God is meek we do not frustrate Him with our sinning to the place where He loses His temper and finally strikes out in anger. He will punish sin and do it justly, but He does it with absolute consideration for mankind. If sin did not have a penalty, God would not be just. If every sin were punished immediately, He would not be merciful. So His meekness strikes that perfect balance between decisiveness and consideration for those He loves and wants to see come to Him in repentance and faith.

When the Apostle Paul faced a matter in the Corinthian church which required discipline, he appealed to them on the basis of "the meekness and gentleness of Christ" (II Corinthians 10:1). Paul had the right as an apostle to make a judgment and boldly command them to obey. But, like Christ, he wanted to give them time to come to the place of obedience by choice rather than by mandate. The church knew that justice had to be done and they knew that Paul would be bold when that time came, but they appreciated his leadership in showing consideration for them as they took "captive every thought to make it obedient to Christ" (II Corinthians 10:5).

This quality of meekness will shine through in all its glory when Christ returns to rule and reign over the entire world. He will bring absolute justice and righteousness, and yet none in His kingdom will need to fear because He will treat every person with loving consideration. His mood will not change depending on circumstances around him. His laws will never need to be revised. Absolute power will be administered with absolute concern.

DARE to enjoy the meekness of God. "Cast all your anxiety on him because he cares for you." (I

Peter 5:7). Take the calendar which you refer to most often in any particular week, whether a physical wall calendar, your Ipad calendar or one on your smart phone. On that calendar write the words "God cares" 365 times, once in the space for every day. No matter how many times you try to convince yourself that no one cares, that every authority in your life is out to punish you and every friend in your life has abandoned you, you will be faced with the unescapable evidence that God cares. He is strong and He is firm. He judges and He punishes sin. But that does not change the fact that He is a meek and gentle God who treats you with perfect consideration and fairness. God is meek.

Dare Thirty-Seven

God is like Water

"LORD, you are the hope of Israel; all who
forsake you will be put to shame. Those who
turn away from you will be written in the dust
because they have forsaken the LORD,
the spring of living water."
Jeremiah 17:13

Taoism likes to illustrate the concept of the
Tao, or the Way, by using the example of water.
"The Tao is like water. Water does not try to impose
its own form on what it encounters but, on the
contrary, is gentle and yielding, fitting into the nooks
and crannies of whatever contains it, yet nothing is
more powerful." (Burke, The Major Religions).
Various writings from Taoism say that the Tao is like

199

water because it seeks the lowest places. It is like water because of the power of gradual influence, turning hills into valleys. The Way is like water because it turns very clear when allowed to simply sit, a picture of the meditation and loss of stress taught in Taoism.

The scriptures also use the illustration of water when teaching us about God. But the reason God is compared to water has nothing to do with humility or power or meditation. The reason God is like water is because water brings life.

Jesus proclaimed Himself as the water of life on the last and greatest days of the feast of Tabernacles (cf. John 7:37-52). For the high priest as well as for the people, the Feast of Tabernacles was one of the greatest holy days of the entire year. The priest would pour out water before the Lord at the brazen altar, a sign of thanksgiving for the rainfall which produced the fertility of the harvest. This water ceremony reminded them of the days of the Exodus when God through Moses provided life-giving water for the children of Israel in the middle of the arid wilderness. It reminded them of the visions of Ezekiel and Zechariah who had seen rivers of healing water flowing out from the temple to heal the land. Zechariah described the event with these words, "On that day a fountain will be opened to the house of David and the inhabitants of Jerusalem, to cleanse them from sin and impurity." (Zechariah 13:1).

The joy of the people as the high priest drew the water from the well and poured it out before the Lord demonstrated their reliance on the temple and the law of Moses. It reminded them they were the people of God. But then, in the midst of their ceremony, a voice rang out. "Let anyone who is thirsty," he shouted, "come to me and drink. Whoever believes in me, as Scripture has said, rivers of living water will flow from within them." (John 7:37-38). The high priest could remind them of the promises of Ezekiel and Zechariah, but Christ was the fulfillment of those promises. Sadly, on that day the high priests and the other leaders of the people refused to see how the very ceremony they were celebrating pointed to the reality of the man who stood before them, the man who had come to give them Himself, the living water.

DARE to drink of God the Living Water. Just as a drink of cold water on a hot summer day quenches physical thirst, so receiving Jesus Christ,

God's Living Water, quenches our spiritual thirst. We will remain thirsty, even if we increase our knowledge of God, unless we receive the Water of Life by faith into our own soul. Christ didn't tell them to think about Him, or to study about Him, or even to declare their love for Him. He told them to drink. Water gives life to plants when absorbed into the inner life of the plant. Men are refreshed physically by water when they take that water into their own bodies. Even so, receiving Christ involves inviting Him to become your Life, the One who gives us what we could never gain for ourselves, divine Life in Him. If you have never received Him, the Water of Life, do it today and then "with joy you will draw water from the wells of salvation." (Isaiah 12:3).

Dare Thirty-Eight

God is Like Rock

"The LORD is my rock, my fortress and my
deliverer; my God is my rock, in whom I take
refuge, my shield and the horn of my
salvation. He is my stronghold, my refuge and
my savior—from violent people you save
me."
II Samuel 22:2-3

The hymn "A Shelter in the Time of Storm"

came from the pen of Vernon Charlesworth who

served as the headmaster of Charles Spurgeon's

Stockwell Orphanage. "The vivid wording of the

hymn assures us that we too are safer during life's

storms with Christ in control than in the calm times

without Him." (Osbeck, "Amazing Grace"). The

words of the hymn came from Old Testament

passages like II Samuel 22:2-3, "The Lord's our

Rock, in Him we hide." But what does it mean to

hide in a rock? Another verse of the hymn speaks of

"a shade by day, defense by night" (Osbeck). Long

before the invention of modern weapons one of the

safest places during a time of battle was the top of a

rock or a rocky hill. Being above the battle enhanced the use of the long-range weapons which were available, spears and arrows and rock-throwing ballistas. Being on top of the rock protected a warrior from hand-to-hand combat.

The writer of II Samuel explains the picture of God as a Rock further by adding words like refuge and stronghold and fortress. A fortress on top of a rock had double protection, being higher than the enemy and standing on a piece of land with rock walls which were hard to scale.

Once again, we are faced with the problem of trying to describe God in terms which are understandable to the human condition. God is not made out of granite, obsidian or marble. He does not physically raise us up to a position higher than our enemies in times of battle. So how is He like a Rock? We are not free in biblical interpretation to simply make up our own ideas of how He is like a Rock. Instead we need to look at the way that picture of God appears in the biblical text. God is like a Rock in that He provides a place of safety, a fortress which cannot be assailed. We find shelter in Him from storms, but that does not mean a tornado will be divinely directed to miss the house where we live. Our shelter involves those spiritual realities which He protects for us.

Anything with us in the Rock fortress is safe. If our joy is in the Rock, our joy is safe from disappointment. But if our joy comes from a source outside the Rock, like our stock portfolio or a beautiful home, He has not promised to protect those. When our love is centered on God the Rock, it will endure forever because His love will never end. Loving this present world will not last because this world will not last. When we trust Him for eternal life, that promise can never fail no matter what enemy we face. Our physical life may suffer even through persecution, but no one will ever be able to triumph against the God-Rock who has guaranteed life in His Son Jesus Christ.

Having God as our Rock does not protect us from the evil which exists in the world, but it does protect us from the evil that once reigned in our hearts. The attacks of the evil one fall harmlessly against the sides of His castle. War may rear its ugly head and affect the nations where believers live, but not even the destruction of war can remove the peace which is found within the walls of His fortress.

Friendships may fail and leave us frustrated and in despair, but the refuge of an everlasting relationship with God will sustain us through the worst of relationship storms.

Our reaction to seeing God like a Rock should be to store up all of our important treasures in Him. Our joy, our peace, our fellowship, our goals, our desires, our friendships, our future and our satisfaction should all be stored inside His fortress where nothing can enter to rob or destroy.

DARE to store your greatest treasures within God the Rock. Pray that God will lay upon your heart the name of one close relative or friend who needs to find shelter within the Rock. Make it your heart's desire to invite them to share an eternal residence in the safety of His fortress. Pray for them. Use every available opportunity to share the love of Christ through your interaction with that person. Give them the gospel in a variety of ways, letting them know of your concern for their soul. Write their name in your notebook and never give up until you know that they are safe inside the Rock and you will never lose their friendship, but instead enjoy it for all eternity.

Dare Thirty-Nine

God as Father

"This, then, is how you should pray:
"'Our Father in heaven,
hallowed be your name,"
Matthew 6:9

When we were living in eastern Montana we knew a family which named each of the boys after western boots like Justin, Dan Post, Lee Miller and Colt Ford. The names identified them as part of a ranch family. But there was an even stronger association when you saw them walk. All of the boys walked just like their father. You could see them from clear across a field and know exactly which family they belonged to just from the way they walked.

The very concept of what it means to be a father comes to us as a reflection of God as Father.

But we must not think that the opposite is also true. The fact that God is called Father should never be based on our ideas of human family relationships. In a human family a father has a son and a son has a father. In the divine relationship the Father has a Son who is the Father. The Son and the Holy Spirit are also One with the Father. The Father would not be God without the Son and the Spirit, just as the Spirit would not be God without the Father and the Son, and the Son would not be God without the Father and the Spirit. They are One, a Perfect Tri-unity.

"The first Jewish rabbi to call God "Father" directly was Jesus of Nazareth. It was a radical departure from tradition, and in fact, in every recorded prayer we have from the lips of Jesus save one, he calls God "Father." (Sproul, "What Does It Mean for Us to Call God our Father?"). God was never seen by the Jewish people as Father even though they had a very well-developed concept of family life. Their relationship with God was based on a national identity, mediated through kings and priests. When God sent Christ the Son to earth, He came in order to become a Mediator who would reconcile man to God and make possible a personal, intimate relationship: adoption as sons (cf. Ephesians 1:5).

The reason we can call God our Father stems from the fact that we have been adopted into His family by faith in the Son of God, Jesus Christ. We are "heirs—heirs of God and co-heirs with Christ, if indeed we share in his sufferings in order that we may also share in his glory." (Romans 8:17). It is only through the Son that any person gains the right to call God Father. The idea of a universal Fatherhood of God which assures universal salvation does not come from the Bible.

Our understanding of God as Father must not come from the example we see in human fathers, even if those fathers are good. A person who refuses to see God as Father because of the failings of a human parent has looked through the wrong end of the telescope. Human fathers must measure up to the example of God and not vice versa.

Our understanding of God as Father also must not come from the human limitations on the concepts of Father, Son and Spirit. Everything Christ said and did is a word and work of God. No separation can occur between them because they are One.

Everything the Holy Spirit does is the work of both the Father and the Son. When the Holy Spirit indwells the believer, Christ indwells the believer. When the Spirit convicts of sin, God convicts of sin. When Christ saves us by faith, salvation is also the work of the Father and the Spirit. When Jesus presents us faultless before the Father, He presents us to Himself.

God as Father is also God as Son and God as Spirit.

DARE to adjust your thinking about God and fatherhood in light of recognizing God as Father. In your notebook make a list of everything you know about God which should be true also of human fathers. Instead of basing what you think about God on what you think of fatherhood, reverse the process. If you are a father, determine to pattern your parenting after the characteristics you see in God the Father. If you struggle with disappointing memories of how you were raised, compare those regrets with the pleasure of sharing sonship with God through Christ, and rejoice in the blessing of knowing God as Father.

Dare Forty

God the Alpha and Omega

"I am the Alpha and the Omega," says the
Lord God,
"who is, and who was, and who is to come,
the Almighty."
Revelation 1:8

Consider all of the different ways people use to describe the limits of time.

Absolutely, all the way, altogether, en masse, exclusively, from A to Z, from beginning to end, fully, in all, from start to finish, from the word go, from end to end, to the nth degree, in entirety, in full, in toto, thoroughly, to the end, to the max, utterly, and wholly.

All these ideas and more are contained in the phrase God uses to describe Himself in the book of Revelation. He is the Alpha and Omega. Nothing comes before Him, and nothing follows after Him.

The phrase comes from the Greek alphabet with Alpha being the first letter and Omega being the last.

Jesus Christ is particularly in view during this vivid description provided in the first chapter of Revelation. In fact, the entire book is called the "Revelation of Jesus Christ" (Rev. 1:1). But we must never forget that in seeing Jesus we are seeing God. The Trinity is One God in Three Persons: Father, Son and Spirit. Everything that is revealed concerning one member of the Tri-unity is also true of the others.

God is the One who inhabits both the beginning and the ending. His attributes include all Divine truth from beginning to end. He is the Absolute, completely true, altogether holy and thoroughly infinite. He is exclusively God, totally different from all others. His mercy, love and grace exist to the nth degree. He is utterly infinite and wholly pure. Any one of His attributes as well as all of them in total can be described by the words Alpha and Omega.

God's description of Himself as the "I AM" (cf. Exodus 3:14) expresses succinctly the summary of His total Being as past, present, future, eternal, infinite and unchangeable. No other came before

212

Him. No other exceeds Him. No other compares with Him. "Rather than give way to doubt and unbelief, let us fall down in lowly adoration at his feet, take His truth, and rejoice in Him as our hope and our everlasting consolation." (Seiss, "The Apocalypse").

DARE to expand your vision of God the Alpha and Omega. On a large blank page draw a time-line of your life. Make it no more than one inch long. At the beginning of the line record your date of birth. Somewhere in the middle of the line write the present date. At the end of the line put a question mark. Now extend the line in each direction but stop before you reach the end of the page. At the left end of the line write Creation. At the right end of the line write Eternity. At this point you have a time-line representing your life and the extent of the created universe in relationship to time. Finally place an arrow at the end of each line extending the line infinitely in both directions. Above the arrow to the left, write Alpha. Above the arrow to the right, write Omega. Take time to focus your mind on the ramifications of your drawing, rejoicing in the truth of God the Alpha and Omega.

Dare Forty-One

God Who Is Enough

"When Abram was ninety-nine years old, the
Lord appeared to him and said, "I am God
Almighty; walk before me faithfully
and be blameless."
Genesis 17:1

King Croesus ruled the land of Lydia and was
one of the first to subjugate the Greeks and make
them pay tribute. Late in his reign he determined to
invade the Persian empire and sought prophetic
advice from the Oracle of Delphi. After offering
lavish gifts to Apollo, the god of Delphi, his
messengers asked the oracle if he should make war
against the Persians. Her famous response was the
ambiguous prophecy, "if Croesus fought against the
Persians, he would bring down a mighty empire."
(Herodotus). Believing his future was assured,
Croesus attacked the Persians and brought down a
mighty empire—his own.

When God announced Himself to Abraham as "God Almighty" in Genesis 17, twenty-five years had passed since the promise of a son had been given to Abram. This new name revealed God as One who possessed might in contrast with the frailty of men. The name could actually mean the God Who is Enough, the All-Sufficient One. God's promise to Abraham concerning the birth of an heir was not ambiguous like the oracle of Delphi. God had promised and He would provide. But at the same time He was assuring Abraham of His all-sufficiency.

The God Who is Enough can provide assurance of His promises. Abraham had been and would continue living a life of faith because the very act of demonstrating that loyalty and trust was his means of finding assurance. Walking by faith and living a righteous life were the result of His trust in God. God gave him promises, but He also provided to Abraham the spiritual desire and spiritual fruit which had been demonstrated during those twenty-five years of delay.

The God Who is Enough also provides hope for the future. Every promise from God to Abraham concerned the future. The land was not going to belong to him, but to his descendants. The seed was a promise of a great nation which would come from him in the future. The blessing was a blessing to the world which would come through his progeny. The All-Sufficiency of God gives hope for a glorious future. We will always have hope when we trust the God Who is Enough.

DARE to commit the future of your family to the God Who is Enough. In your notebook, write out a one hundred year "hope" for your children and later descendants. Plan the godly future you would like to have them experience. Ask God to give your children, grandchildren and great-grandchildren godly spouses. Ask Him to be preparing right now the parents of those who will one day marry your descendants so that those parents will raise the future spouses in the nurture and admonition of the Lord. Outline the education you would like your children, grandchildren and great-grandchildren to receive. Ask God to prepare spiritual mentors, godly teachers and strong Christian institutions which will be in place when those from your family begin school and go all the way through graduate degrees. Make your plans as specific as possible, committing all the plans to the All-Sufficiency of Almighty God. Specify the type of church community experience you would like them to enjoy. Pray for those who are right now in the process of theological training who will one day serve as the pastors of those churches. Pray for the countries where your descendants will live and the communities where they will make their homes. Look to the future, even beyond this life you live on earth, and trust that future to the promises of God.

Dare Forty-Two

God Who Cares

"Cast all your anxiety on him because
he cares for you."
I Peter 5:7

There is a Chinese parable which tells of a woman who lost her only son. She was so grief-stricken that it was said she made her sorrow her wailing wall. Finally she went to a wise philosopher who told her he would give her back her son if she would bring him a mustard seed from a home where there has never been any sorrow. Eagerly she started her search, going from home to home in search of the mustard seed which would bring back her son. In every case she learned that sorrow had come to that home. Finally, she returned to the philosopher, empty-handed but no longer grieving. She admitted to him that she had been selfish in her grief because sorrow is common to all.

If that lesson, that sorrow is common to all, were all that we knew about God, we would be of all men most miserable. What we do know about God is that He cares for those who sorrow. That one fact about God raises us from the depressing prospect of sorrow entering each life to the amazing truth that God has lessons for us to learn even from the school of sorrow.

The sorrow of hard work can teach us the value of love. The story of Jacob recorded in Genesis 29 reveals the life of a man who enrolled in the school of sorrow for more than twenty years. Jacob worked seven years to earn the hand of Rachel in marriage but "they seemed like only a few days to him because of his love for her" (Genesis 29:20). Laban did not treat his potential son-in-law with kindness. The work was hard and in the end, because of Laban's trickery, he was actually going to work fourteen years for Rachel. But love made that hard work seem easy.

The love of God is also what made the tremendously hard work of facing the cross bearable for our Savior. "For the joy set before him he endured the cross, scorning its shame, and sat down at the right hand of the throne of God." (Hebrews 12:2). In the same manner our hardships related to our work for God demonstrate the value we place on our relationship with Him.   Generations of persecuted believers give testimony to the fact that suffering for the cause of Christ can be born with patience because of love.

The sorrow of unjust treatment can also teach us the value of honesty. In the earlier story of Jacob's life he had been known as a trickster. His father had even succumbed to his deceit and given him the blessing. But he finally met his match in Laban who consistently promised one thing and then did the bait and switch.   The result of Laban's actions brought sorrow to the entire family, from antagonism between the two sisters to strife and even murder in the lives of their children.

Sometimes Bible stories are recorded to teach us what is not true about God. What God wanted Jacob to learn from Laban's deception and the injustice he endured was trust in the One who is holy, the One who is never unjust. Jacob stole his brother's blessing. He worked hard for Laban's blessing which never came, but in the end he was able to set aside all of his trust in men and say to God, "I will not let you go, unless you bless me" (Genesis 32:26). He finally learned to turn away from seeking the approval of all others in order to desire the blessing of the One who truly cares.

DARE to cast all your cares upon Him. The greatest physical evidence of God's care for us comes from the cross of Christ. In His death He demonstrated a care far beyond any comfort or compassion we could ever receive or share with others. As a symbol of your desire to cast your cares upon Him, plant a "Cares Garden." Every time you face another sorrow, place a miniature cross in the garden. The fact that sorrow enters into every life may soon result in a garden of crosses which rivals Arlington National Cemetery. But every cross will be another reminder that no matter the size or the frequency of sorrow in this life, we have a God who cares.

Dare Forty-Three

God in the Shadows

"He inquired of the Lord, but the Lord did not
answer him
by dreams or Urim or prophets."
I Samuel 28:6

James Russell Lowell struggled most of his life with the doubts and frustrations of an existence that seemed to be lived with a God who was distant. He married the sister of one of his classmates at Harvard and the couple had four children, but only one survived infancy. He saw his nation moving toward an inevitable struggle over slavery and became deeply involved in the advocacy of abolition. His poem "The Present Crisis" which later became the hymn "Once To Every Man and Nation," was written to protest the war with Mexico. Lowell felt, along with Abraham Lincoln and others, that increasing American possessions in that area would "increase the power of the southern states and enlarge the area in which slavery was accepted." (Cottrill, "Hymns of the Church").

"Once to every man and nation, Comes the moment
to decide,
In the strife of truth with falsehood, For the good or
evil side;
Some great cause, some great decision, Offering each
the bloom or blight,
And the choice goes by forever, 'Twixt that darkness
and that light."
"Though the cause of evil prosper, Yet the truth alone
is strong;
Though her portion be the scaffold, And upon the
throne be wrong;
Yet that scaffold sways the future, And behind the
dim unknown,
Standeth God within the shadow, Keeping watch
above His own."

James Russell Lowell

There is no doubt that when Daniel and the other boys from Jerusalem were being marched off to Babylon as captives there were many of them who felt God had faded away into the shadows. The cause of evil was prospering and wrong was certainly on the throne. But in the first chapter of the book of Daniel we see four young men who, when faced with the loss of family, friends and freedom, remained confident that their future was still under the control of God within the shadows.

The fact that God was still in control caused them to do everything they could to work with Him. They yielded to His control and made choices that supported what they knew God wanted from them. These four boys worked hard at interpersonal relationships, but at the same time it was God who "caused the official to show favor" (Daniel 1:9). The favor shown them by the official recognized their inner character. It came as a result of the fact that he appreciated the humility in Daniel's request. It honored their personal and private faith. What the official saw in them caused him to grant the permission they requested, but the four of them knew that it was God in the shadows who worked all things together for their good.

Daniel and his friends also worked hard at their studies while recognizing at the same time that "God gave knowledge and understanding of all kinds of literature and learning" (Daniel 1:17). They showed that it was possible to study academic knowledge without abandoning God's knowledge. They excelled in their understanding of subjects taught by their Chaldean rulers while at the same time retaining their faith in God. When their education was complete they had the wisdom to participate in an earthly kingdom without forsaking God's kingdom. In that position they demonstrated a wisdom superior to others without forgetting that it was a gift from God. What a testimony to their awareness that even when He seemed to be out of sight, God was standing in the shadows keeping watch above his own.

DARE to see God in the shadows. Societal relationships, education and politics in our day all seem determined to push God further into the shadows of popular culture. Create a piece of artwork depicting one of our national buildings or monuments: the Capital, White House, Mount Rushmore, Lincoln Memorial or some other famous landmark. Show that monument casting a shadow over the rest of the nation, but within the shadow include imagery which reveals God, ignored and yet active on behalf of His own.

Dare Forty-Four

God at Work

"Being confident of this, that he who began a
good work in you will carry it on to
completion until the day of Christ Jesus."
Philippians 1:6

It is not uncommon for a large fence to be
placed around a worksite. In some places, however,
windows will be included in the fence so that those
who are interested can look in and see what is being
accomplished. Those who drive by and simply see
the fence may conclude that nothing is happening, but
those who stop to take a closer look realize that the
project inside the fence is taking shape.

God did not quit working after the six days of
creation. He rested on the Sabbath day to provide
man with an example of His plan for work and

227

worship. But He then continued to work and still continues to work today. Sometimes we travel through life right alongside a great work which God is undertaking and never even notice what He is doing. The story in Genesis of how God worked to provide for the family of Jacob, even without their knowledge, reveals some important principles which should open our eyes to God at work (cf. Genesis 42-43).

We miss seeing God at work when we close our minds to the unthinkable. Jacob and his sons knew there was corn in Egypt. But to them it was unthinkable that God had prepared that corn for them. They never even considered the possibility that Joseph might be in the picture, used by God to preserve their lives. Jacob would have been quick to assert that God could do miracles. But believing that God had the ability to do the miraculous was entirely different from thinking that He had already done the unthinkable.

We will never see God at work until we accept the inexplicable. There were several events in the story of Joseph and his brothers which they could not explain. These events should have opened their eyes so they could see God at work, but they didn't. They could not explain why an Egyptian governor would want to see their youngest brother. They had no idea why an Egyptian ruler would tell them that he feared God (Genesis 42:18). He assured them on the basis of his faith in God that he would not harm them if they left one brother behind and brought the youngest brother to Egypt. That should have opened their eyes.

We will never see God at work until we learn to accept His blessings. Joseph fills their sacks with corn. He returns their money to them. He gives them provisions to eat on the way back home. But instead of seeing this as a blessing they somehow turn it around to the conclusion that God was punishing them in some way. When they get back to Jacob all they can remember is that they were treated roughly. The blessings they received should have shown them that God was at work.

We will never see God at work unless we let go of the past. Although God exists apart from time, He never goes back and changes our past. That is a science fiction anomaly which will never occur. Instead He enables us to accept the past and trust Him for the future. When the brothers tell Jacob that they need to have Benjamin accompany them on their next trip to Egypt, he clings to his bereavement, the promise that he would go to his grave mourning for Joseph. He reveals his distrust of his other sons, based on a strong feeling that they had never told him the truth about Joseph and would bring Benjamin into mischief as well. He descends into despair even though it means leaving Simeon in Egypt and the entire family starving when the present store of corn is depleted. But those reactions to the past actually kept him from the realization of his greatest desire, to see Joseph again. And all the time God was just waiting to bless him abundantly above all he could ask or think, because God was at work.

DARE to see God at work in your own life. B. M. Franklin has written a poem called "The Weaver" which includes these lines.

> "Oft times He weaveth sorrow
> And I, in foolish pride,
> Forget He sees the upper,
> And I the under side."

Purchase, or better yet, create your own weaving. Notice how the pattern or picture on the top seems perfect and undisturbed while the back side of the weaving contains knots and a collection of colors which seem to have no pattern or design. As you face sorrow, bereavement and disappointment in your life, use the weaving to remind you that the knots and discolorations you presently experience are in the hands of God producing a picture, the "good work in you" (Phil. 1:6) which He will carry to completion. God is at work in you.

Dare Forty-Five

God and History

"O king, the Most High God gave your father
Nebuchadnezzar sovereignty
and greatness and glory and splendor."
Daniel 5:18

Not long after the attacks on the World Trade Center in 2001 an Egyptian pop singer wrote a song blaming the attacks on Israel and the United States itself. Since that time others throughout the Middle East have rewritten history in the same way, saying that 9/11 was basically an inside job so that the United States would have an excuse to attack Iraq and Afghanistan. We have come to expect such revisionist history from Islamic extremists.

Sadly, history narrators for many years have ignored the role God plays in the story of humanity. When Daniel faced Belshazzar as recorded in Daniel

5 he tried to teach him some very important lessons about the role God plays in historical events. Understanding the role God plays in history will be a tremendous aid in our development of a greater understanding of God Himself.

When God looks at history He sees Himself at work. There is a perspective on history which has the capacity to transform a dreary study of dates and times into one of the most interesting subjects we will ever investigate. That perspective comes when we begin to see history as a record of God at work. There are those who think that God has not worked since the days of creation. They believe He set the world in motion like a clock and has simply been allowing it to run on its own ever since. Daniel wanted Belshazzar to know that his own history was a work of God. God had given Nebuchadnezzar the kingdom and along with it majesty and glory and honor. When we see God at work in history we will notice not only what He gives to people but also what He chooses not to give. Belshazzar had been given the same kingdom as Nebuchadnezzar, but he possessed none of the majesty, glory and honor. History books for many years didn't even recognize that Belshazzar existed. Not all who rule are equal, but all those who rule attain their positions because of the sovereign work of God.

When God looks at history He sees men as they really are. There is a very real difference between a biography and an autobiography. A man may set out to write a very honest record of his own life, but in an autobiography there will always be stories omitted because they are too embarrassing and accounts elaborated which make that person look good. A well-written biography will deal honestly with both the good and the bad in a person's life. God gives us honest biographies, history without the spin man would add if he were writing it himself. The spiritual condition of Belshazzar and his pride was portrayed honestly. "You have not humbled yourself, though you knew all this," Daniel rebukes him. "You have set yourself up against the Lord of heaven." (Daniel 5:22-23).

When God looks at history He sees men as they will be. The handwriting on the wall of the palace revealed exactly what Belshazzar would face in the immediate future. His worth had been counted out, weighed, and found to be lacking in value. God had measured the job the king was doing and decided it was time to bring the Babylonian kingdom to an end. He had placed Belshazzar on the scales of justice and discovered just how inadequate his performance had been. Now the kingdom was going to be divided between the Medes and the Persians.

When we look at history never forget that it is His Story and that He wants to make His Story our story as well.

DARE to see God at work in all of history. Obtain a copy of the largest Sunday newspaper in the locale where you live. Read the paper in its entirety, from the first page to the last. With a highlighter mark or underline every instance you see of God at work. If you don't see God at work on every page of the newspaper, go through it again. Look behind the reporting to what is really taking place. Watch to see men revealed as they really are, either rebelling against God or responding to Him. Read carefully to see God at work showing men as they will be. Power, greatness, glory and honor are still given by God. Remember that not every person who has power also has glory and honor. Not every person considered great possesses real power. There are many who receive honor but do not deserve glory. In the end every person will need to give account of himself or herself to God (cf. Romans 14:12). Train yourself to see God at work in all of history, including today's newspaper or newscast.

Dare Forty-Six

A God of Honor

"(Now Jesus himself had pointed out that a
prophet has no honor in his own country.)"
John 4:44

The highest military honor given by the
United States for personal acts of valor beyond the
call of duty is the Medal of Honor. Former Army
soldier Robert Dale Maxwell received the medal for
actions during World War II. "When an enemy hand
grenade was thrown in the midst of his squad,
Technician 5th Grade Maxwell unhesitatingly hurled
himself squarely upon it, using his blanket and his
unprotected body to absorb the full force of the
explosion. This act of instantaneous heroism
permanently maimed Technician 5th Grade Maxwell,
but saved the lives of his comrades in arms and

239

facilitated maintenance of vital military communications during the temporary withdrawal of the battalion's forward headquarters." (military.com).

It is entirely right for us as a nation to honor our heroes. Pledging allegiance to the flag and standing respectfully when the national anthem is sung express visually our recognition of the debt of gratitude we owe to those who have fought and died to obtain our freedom.

But even the honor we owe to our national heroes pales in comparison to the respect, gratitude and appreciation we owe to the God of Honor. The Ten Commandments begin with the strong admonition to accord Him the honor He deserves. No other god is to be honored above Him. He is not to be reduced to the level of being represented by the image of anything He has created. He alone deserves all our worship. His name must always be held in the highest esteem and His day of worship must be sacred above all other days (cf. Exodus 20:1-8).

When Jesus stated that no prophet receives the honor he deserves in his own country, He made reference to the fact that people find it hard to honor those who are familiar to them. There were people who followed Christ, heard Him preach and even saw His miracles who did not give Him honor. Just before making this statement He had been honored as the Son of God in Samaria (cf. John 4:42). The Samaritans were the last people anyone in Galilee or Judea would have expected to welcome Him as the Messiah. But they had done that while His own people refused to honor Him.

They had witnessed His miracles, but that was not enough to cause them to honor Him. They had experienced His compassion and faithfulness in the meeting of personal needs in people whom they knew well. But they still refused to see Him as the God of Honor. A person who honors Christ simply because they believe He can satisfy personal needs has a self-centered religion. Such a person reduces God to their own ATM instead of granting Him the honor He deserves as Lord and Master. When that person doesn't get from God what they think they deserve, the honor ends.

True honor to God comes from those who place their complete trust in Him, having faith in Him and nothing else, knowing that He alone will keep them all the way through eternity. That is the kind of honor the God of Honor deserves.

DARE to worship the God of Honor.

For the next four weeks clear your calendar so that you can dedicate a twelve-hour day once each week to worshipping the God of Honor. On that day seek a place where you can be completely alone with God. Resolve to spend the entire twelve hours in just three activities: reading the Bible, praying and contemplating the knowledge of God. Walk if you need to in order to stay alert. Read aloud from the Scriptures. Pray aloud as well as silently. Think about every attribute of God you can recall from this study and invite God to reveal Himself to you more perfectly. Give Him the honor He deserves as the God of Honor.

Dare Forty-Seven

God the Good Shepherd

"I am the good shepherd. The good shepherd
lays down his life for the sheep."
John 10:11

The Jewish Festival of Hanukkah began at the
time of the Maccabean revolt against the Greeks.
When the Maccabean army gained control of the city
of Jerusalem they immediately set about to cleanse
the temple, which had been spiritually defiled. The
method they chose was to burn ritual oil in the temple
menorah for eight days. But they discovered that they
only had enough oil for one day. They lit the
menorah anyway and to their amazement that small
amount of oil lasted the full eight days (Chabad.org).

Hanukkah is not one of the festivals instituted by Moses in the law, but it was part of the religious heritage of the Jewish people in the time of Christ. Its focus was on the failure of political and religious leadership and the need for good shepherds to lead the people in the ways of God. That was exactly what Jesus had come to do. In John 10 He takes the occasion of a great holiday celebration and turns the attention of the crowd toward Himself. He is the shepherd they need. He is the One who will lead their nation back to God.

Seeing God as the Good Shepherd introduces us to some very practical ways in which He becomes involved with our lives. God is a completely trustworthy Shepherd. History is replete with stories of political leaders who came to power with promises of sharing wealth with the people, righting wrongs and establishing justice only to fall into the same patterns of greed and extortion which characterized the regimes they replaced. God is not like those leaders who preyed upon the sheep because they were "thieves and robbers" (John 10:8). He will never lead us astray or deceive us. He is truthful, One who cannot tell a lie. His involvement in our lives does not involve taking something from us because He has need of nothing. Instead of robbing from us, His goal is to make us spiritually rich.

God the Good Shepherd cares for us. The picture in John is of a shepherd who personally sleeps at the opening of the sheepfold in order to protect his flock. He is not like those who seek leadership in order to "kill and destroy" (John 10:10). Instead He promises abundant life now and eternal life hereafter. He doesn't destroy but instead builds us up by changing us into His own image with ever-increasing glory (cf. II Corinthians 3:18).

God the Good Shepherd transforms us. The relationship between the sheep and the Shepherd changes the sheep as they follow the path where He leads. They learn to hear His voice and respond to Him. He knows them by name and as a result leads them in the very best path, a journey which they could never even begin to imagine on their own. He gives abundant life, expanding horizons and leading his sheep into realms of adventure they would never explore without His guidance. He teaches His sheep to know Him intimately, the pattern for this knowledge being the intimate relationship between the Father and the Son (cf. John 10:15). Nothing will transform a person more than the process of coming to know God in a greater fashion day by day. We can be changed into His image. His love can become our love. His grace can become our grace. His joy can become our joy. His peace can become our peace.

DARE to follow the path laid out by God the Good Shepherd. Obtain the other four books in this series. Allow the path of His Word to guide your steps into a transformational life. See how you can be "Transformed by God." Recognize the privilege of participating in His work by "Serving God." Open your eyes to the adventure and thrill of being "Creative Like God." Embark on the continuing journey of Walking on Water by daily exploring His Word through "Dare to Walk on Water: The Workbook." A transformed future awaits you as you follow God the Good Shepherd.

Dare Forty-Eight

God the Judge

"Far be it from you to do such a thing--to kill
the righteous with the wicked, treating the
righteous and the wicked alike. Far be it from
you! Will not the Judge of all the earth do
right?"
Genesis 18:25

Imagine that the next seven days are going to
take you to the highest plateau and the lowest
emotional depths you have ever experienced. What if
you could see the future and know that by the middle
of this week your closest friend would be lauded in a
ticker tape parade down Broadway in New York City,
and you would be right there with him. And then,
two days later, that same friend would be executed on
public television, tried, judged and publicly
condemned to death. Instead of enjoying a life of

247

prestige and power as one of his friends, you would be running for your life, in fear of the authorities who arrested him.

That scene describes the experiences facing Christ's disciples in chapter 18 of the book of Luke. As Jesus prepared His disciples for the terrible week to come He taught them an important lesson concerning how to handle delay, how to face disappointment. As Luke introduces the parable, often called the "Parable of the Unjust Judge," he tells us exactly why Jesus shared the story at that time, "to show them that they should always pray and not give up" (Luke 18:1). During any delay in our lives we have two options. Either we persevere in prayer or we give up. By the end of the Passion Week, when they were faced with the reality of His death on the cross, when they were emotionally distraught to the place where they were hiding in fear for their own lives, they could persevere in prayer or they could give up.

This parable is different from many of the other stories Jesus told. In most of the parables Jesus taught by comparison, but here He teaches by contrast. Everything we learn about God the Judge in

248

this parable is in complete contrast to what we learn about the unjust judge. The unjust judge was totally unprincipled simply because he did not have any respect or fear of God. His dispensing of justice was limited to what he determined to be right or wrong because He did not have God's wisdom.

When God rules as a Judge that ruling is always just. He will never arrive at the wrong conclusion. He will never be persuaded by bribes. He will never treat the righteous and the wicked alike. He is the Judge of all the world and He will do right.

The unjust judge was indifferent to the plight of the widow, even though widows were entitled to special care and protection under the Law (cf. Deut. 27:19). He knew that requirement of the Law or he would not have been a judge. He knew what the Law said, He knew what God expected him to do, but he didn't care.

God is not like the unjust judge. He will always keep His Word. In fact it is on the basis of the Word of God that His judgements will be made. "There is a judge for the one who rejects me and does not accept my words; the very words I have spoken will condemn them at the last day" (John 12:48). The reason we can trust the Word of God stems from the fact that God Himself can be trusted. Every promise He has made in the Bible will be fulfilled.

God is not like the unjust judge because the judge could be annoyed into granting requests simply because he was self-centered. The only reason he ever helped the widow was because he wanted to get rid of her. God does not answer prayer to get rid of us. We must never think that we annoy God into answering our requests. We are not persistent in prayer because we think God can be persuaded by our pleading. Prayer is not a way that we manipulate God into giving us health and wealth and prosperity. We persist in prayer because we have come to believe that God has a reason for everything He does, including delays. If we don't accept that truth, then the only other option is to give up.

Persistence in prayer does not change the length of a delay, it changes us so that we recognize and trust a God who always has a reason for His delays. It means that we learn to trust Him even when we do not understand what He is doing. We pray because we are convinced that God the Judge will do what is right.

DARE to pray with complete trust in God the Judge. Add a page to your notebook with the title Prayer Requests. Divide the page into three columns. In the first column write out your prayer requests in enough detail that you will know when they have been answered. In the second column write the answer to those prayers when they are received. Don't limit your answers to what you perceive to be positive. That is, don't record only the answers which satisfy you. If God says "no" record the "no." Then in the third column, after the answer has come, write "God was right." Dare to allow Him to change you into that disciple who is convinced that God the Judge will always do what is right.

Dare Forty-Nine

God's House

"He was afraid and said, "How awesome is
this place! This is none other
than the house of God; this is the gate of
heaven."
"He called that place Bethel,"
Genesis 28:17, 19

Perhaps you remember going to church as a child and being told not to run in the aisles, climb over the pews, chew gum or ever laugh out loud because you were in God's house. Based on all we have learned about God there are several obvious truths concerning such behavior which we should know. Although we use the term God's house to refer to a church building "the Most High does not live in houses made by human hands" (Acts 7:48). God does not stay in a church building when we leave so that we can come back and visit Him the next

Sunday. He had a special presence in the Jewish Temple represented by His Shekinah glory, and the temple was called the house of God, but even the temple did not contain God in the way we think of living in a house. When Jacob met God in a dream he called the place Bethel, meaning God's house, simply because God was there. So anyplace we meet with God can be called God's house.

In Genesis 35 Jacob returned to Bethel. The entire chapter records what happened when he returned to the place where he had previously met with God. Those same experiences can happen to us as we meet with God, no matter the location.

When we go to God's house we will listen closely to the voice of God. Jacob heard from God in a dream and we hear from Him through His Word, but the result should be the same. Whether in a church service or in our own personal devotional time, our attitude matters. Meeting with God provides an opportunity to sit and listen to Him. We should desire and value such communication.

Visiting in God's house will cause us to clean up our personal lifestyle. Jacob instructed his entire household to put away false gods and physically purify themselves in anticipation of meeting with God (cf. Genesis 35:2). Washing themselves and changing clothes was simply an outward display of reverence for God. What really mattered was their inward, spiritual cleansing. Every great revival the world has ever seen has been accompanied by a moral renewal in society.

When we go back to Bethel, the house of God, we will remember His provision for us in the past. Perhaps one of the greatest problems we face as believers is the curse of a short memory. Meeting with God should remind us of the long list of blessings He has already gifted to us, the blessing of godly ancestors, prayer warriors, freedom to worship, the transforming influence of the gospel, and a multitude of other memories.

Spending time in God's house will cause us to become known by the strength of our God. For Jacob that brought safety in the face of military enemies (cf. Genesis 35:5). They were not afraid of the sons of Jacob, they were afraid of the God of Jacob. We too will enjoy the protection of God when we understand what it means to hold Him in absolute reverence, in holy awe, when we fear Him and so fear doing those foolish things that dishonor Him. We think that God is somehow diminished when people in the church fail. Nothing could be farther from the truth. We are diminished by our failure to stay in fellowship with Him. Dwelling in His house will be our strength.

Going back to Bethel will result in worship. Jacob built an altar (cf. Gen. 35:7). He named it "El-Bethel" meaning the God of the house of God. When His people meet, whether in the middle of the wilderness, in the temple or in a church building, He should be worshipped. A local body of believers, banded together for mutual edification, exhortation and comfort is the way God planned for His people to experience corporate worship in the present age.

Dwelling in the house of God will result in God's blessing (cf. Gen. 35:9). His promises will become real in our lives. In Bethel Jacob could see the future God had planned for him in a way he could never envision while under the thumb of Laban. Fellowship with God should open our eyes to the possibilities in store for us as we follow the path of righteousness God has planned for each one of us.

DARE to go back to Bethel, dare to take up residence in the house of God. We know that church is not the only place we meet with God. But for the next four weeks work to extend the time you spend in the building where your local body of believers meets for worship. Go to church at least a half hour before service begins. Find a place in the auditorium where you can read your Bible and engage in silent prayer. Use that time to prepare your own heart for a willing reception of God's Word. Remain in place after the service, perhaps even another half an hour, thinking about what you have learned and seeking strength from the Lord to apply it to your own heart and life. Remind yourself that "we are the temple of the living God. As God has said: 'I will live with them and walk among them, and I will be their God, and they will be my people" (II Corinthians 6:16). Learn what it means to dwell in His house constantly.

Dare Fifty

Jesus is God

"And from Jesus Christ, who is the faithful
witness, the firstborn from the dead, and the
ruler of the kings of the earth. To him who
loves us and has freed us from our sins by his
blood, and has made us to be a kingdom and
priests to serve his God and Father--to him be
glory and power for ever and ever! Amen."
Revelation 1:5-6

Imagine yourself as the teacher of a third
grade class full of boys who caused the second grade
teacher the year before to resign in despair. But
within the class is one boy who is different. He
doesn't say much, but he works hard, and speaks
respectfully. You wish you had more time to spend
with him, but with a class like that it is just not
possible. Now jump ahead forty years. You have just
begun to enjoy your retirement when you receive an
invitation to the inauguration of a new president. You

have not seen him in forty years, but you immediately recognize the name—the boy from your third-grade class. He remains soft-spoken and respectful, but now you see him in an entirely different light than before. You now see him no longer a boy, but the man who holds the most powerful office on earth.

The Apostle John had a similar experience. He had known Jesus during the incarnation, walked with him on the dusty roads of Israel. He had heard Him preach, seen the miracles and taken Mary into his own house in response to Jesus' request from the cross. He had witnessed the resurrection and had been there on the Mount the day Christ ascended. Now, on the island of Patmos he sees Him again, not in the flesh but in the glory. He sees Jesus, and in seeing Jesus he sees God.

John sees Jesus as God the Judge, in the clothes of a High Priest, the supreme judge of God's system of legal justice (cf. Rev. 1:13). He is clothed from head to foot in robes which set Him apart from all others. He appears in the midst of His church, the golden candlesticks, with supreme authority and awesome majesty.

John sees Jesus as the Eternal God. His description matches that of the Ancient of Days seen by the prophet Daniel (cf. Rev. 1:14, Daniel 7:22). Jesus is the everlasting, the eternal, the infinite Son of God. As One with God He is unlimited, ageless, eternally pure and omnisciently wise.

John sees Jesus as the All-seeing God. Human eyes shine only with reflected light. But the eyes of the Son of God were like a "blazing fire" (Rev. 1:14). The light of His eyes came from within. Here was the glance that brought to light the hidden things of darkness. Here was the gaze before which all things became naked and open. God's flaming eyes look right into the hearts of men and know their thoughts and intents. Nothing is hidden from Him.

John sees Jesus as the God of holiness. His feet of brass glowed like metal heated to the place of whiteness. It was painful to the eyes to even try to look on them from a distance. God is the God of holiness, whom none can approach except through the One who Himself is holy.

John sees Jesus as the God of Judgment. When He comes again and every eye sees Him, He will not be coming as the Suffering Savior, but as the

Omnipotent Judge. He will come in overwhelming glory, pure-white holiness, transcendent splendor and incomparable majesty. There will be no doubt in the mind of any person that Jesus is God.

DARE to see Jesus as God. It is one thing to read through the gospels and be reminded that everything Jesus did was an action of God. It was God who lay in the manger, God who walked on water and God who prayed in the garden of Gethsemane. It was God who died for our sin and God who rose from the dead. All of that is true and all of that is important to our understanding of God.

But when we think about Jesus we also need to think about Him as God outside of the period of His incarnation. Go back to the table of contents and look at every characteristic and action we have studied concerning God. Rewrite the table of contents in your notebook replacing every occurrence of the word God with the word Jesus. Forget the Jesus you have created in your human mind and see the Son of God revealed in the Bible. Jesus is without limits. Jesus is the uncreated. Jesus is love. Jesus is transcendent. Jesus never changes. Jesus is life. JESUS IS GOD!

Dare Fifty-One

Holy Spirit is God

"Then Peter said, "Ananias, how is it that
Satan has so filled your heart that you have
lied to the Holy Spirit and have kept for
yourself some of the money you received for
the land? Didn't it belong to you before it was
sold? And after it was sold, wasn't the money
at your disposal? What made you think of
doing such a thing? You have not lied just to
human beings but to God."
Acts 5:3-4

In preparation for acting the part of Sherlock
Holmes an actor grew a mustache and dyed his blond
hair a dark black. His three-year-old granddaughter,
who adored her Papa, would have nothing to do with
him until the mustache came off and the hair color
was restored. She could not believe that he was still
the same person.

Sometimes our perception of the Holy Spirit suffers from the same misconception of perception. We can believe that God the Father and God the Son are One and the same, but the Holy Spirit seems so different. The truth is that all three are One and all three possess every attribute, share every characteristic and perform every work in complete Unity.

The Holy Spirit is clearly identified as God in the fifth chapter of the book of Acts. Peter told Ananias he had lied to the Holy Spirit and that he had lied to God. In Acts 28:25-27 Paul tells us that what God said in Isaiah 6 was the word of the Holy Spirit as well.

The Holy Spirit possesses the same attributes as God, Eternality (cf. Hebrews 9:14), Omnipresence (cf. Psalm 139:7-10), Omniscience (cf. I Corinthians 2:10-11), Omnipotence (cf. Genesis 1:2), and Holiness (cf. Psalm 51:11).

The Holy Spirit performs the same works as God. He took part in creation when "the Spirit of God was hovering over the waters" (Genesis 1:2). He regenerates, actively imparting spiritual life to those who trust in God. "He saved us through the washing of rebirth and renewal by the Holy Spirit" (Titus 3:5). The Holy Spirit inspired Scripture, superintending in the lives of the writers, "For prophecy never had its origin in the human will, but prophets, though human, spoke from God as they were carried along by the Holy Spirit" (II Peter 1:21). The Holy Spirit was active as God in the resurrection of Jesus. "And if the Spirit of him who raised Jesus from the dead is living in you, he who raised Christ from the dead will also give life to your mortal bodies because of his Spirit who lives in you" (Acts 8:11). It is also the Holy Spirit who is at work in the sanctification of the believer. "But we ought always to thank God for you, brothers and sisters loved by the Lord, because God chose you as firstfruits to be saved through the sanctifying work of the Spirit and through belief in the truth" (II Thess. 2:13).

DARE to see the Holy Spirt as God. In your notebook reproduce the table of contents once again. This time substitute the words Holy Spirit for every time the word God is used. As you do this exercise, think about what it means in your own life for the indwelling Spirit of God to be identical with God. Forget the Holy Spirit you created in your human mind. See God the Holy Spirit as infinite, true, holy, omniscient, love, and peace. See Him as One who never sleeps, who cares for us and who is Enough. THE HOLY SPIRIT IS GOD.

Dare Fifty-Two

God is God

"Remember the former things, those of long
ago; I am God, and there is no other; I am
God, and there is none like me."
Isaiah 46:9

In the science of Bible translation there is a
Greek term called hapax legomena which means that
a particular word occurs only once in the entire New
Testament. When we think of something unique we
may use the illustration of fingerprints or individual
snowflakes. But the fact that God alone is God
cannot be compared to being a fingerprint different
from all other fingerprints or a snowflake different
from all other snowflakes. He is not just a God
different from all other gods. A better comparison

would be to a hapax legomenon, the only and completely unique use of a word in an entire work of literature. God alone is God. There is no one else like Him. No other can be compared to Him or even occupy the same category as He inhabits.

No other being is a God without Limits.

No other being is God in Tri-Unity.

No other being is God, the Uncreated.

There is no other God Who Needs Nothing.

None other is like Him in beauty.

None other is an Eternal God.

No other being is an Infinite God.

None other can claim to be a God Who Never

Changes.

No other being is God Immaterial.

There is nothing else who is God is Life

Nothing else in the universe knows all.

Only God is All-Wise.

Nothing can replace God our Refuge.

There is no other source of joy except God our

Joy.

No other is God Transcendent.

God is the only source of Light.

None can compare to God Omnipresent.

No other God is Faithful.

None but God is Good.

There is none other like God who is Just.

There is none other like God in Mercy.

There is none other like God who is Love.

Only God is Holy.

Only God is Sovereign.

Only God is Truth.

Only God is Almighty.

No other being like God is Grace.

None other compares to God who is Gentle.

None other compares to God who is

Longsuffering.

There is no other God of Peace.

Only God is Self-Controlled.

Only God is Meek.

There is only one God Who is Enough.

None other cares like God Cares.

None other works like God at Work.

Nothing like God exists in all of History.

No other deserves honor like the God of

Honor.

No one compares to God the Good Shepherd.

No one will ever excel God the Judge.

DARE to treasure God, the only God. Never allow any other to replace Him. Value His love above any other love. Depend on His wisdom above any other wisdom. Participate in His work with greater energy than any other work. Honor Him above any other hero. Bow to His sovereignty before any other sovereign. Adore His beauty above any other beauty. Seek His peace above any other peace.

Desire His holiness above any other standard of holiness. Be satisfied with joy from Him above any other joy.

Dare to Walk on Water – Treasuring God!

OTHER BOOKS IN THIS SERIES

"Dare to Walk on Water: Creative Like God"

Dare to Walk on Water: Serving God"

Dare to Walk on Water: Transformed by God

Dare to Walk on Water: The Workbook

The four Dare to Walk on Water devotionals and the workbook can be used in any order. Read the devotionals a day at a time or spend an entire week on each chapter, taking time to put into action the adventures awaiting you as you experience the power of the Word of God at work in your own life. DARE to move beyond devotional Christianity to creative Christianity, daily transformed into the image of the Son of God, Jesus Christ.

BIBLIOGRAPHY

"The Absent-Minded Professor" Walt Disney Films, 1961.

Allen, Robert, "Theosmusica," Kindle Publishing, 2015.

Anderson, Bernhard, "Out of the Depths," Westminster, Philadelphia, PA. 1983.

Bellinger, W. H., "Psalms" Baker, GrandRapids, MI. 2012.

Bright, Brad, discovergod.com., Campus Crusade for Christ, 2016.

Burke, T. Patrick, The Major Religions, Blackwell Publishing, Malden, MA 2004.

"Chanukah (Hanakkuh)" Chabad.org. n.d.

Cotrill, Robert, "Once To Every Man and Nation," Hymns of the Church, wordwisehymns.com., November 21, 2011.

Croswell, Ken, "Farthest confirmed galaxy is a prolific star creator," Physics World, Oct. 23, 2013.

Dickens, Charles, "A Christmas Carol," Top Five Books, LLC, Oak Park, IL, 2011.

"Did Yuri Gagarin Say He Didn't See God In Space?" Valentin Petrov, Pravmir.com., April 12, 2013.

"Early History," Women's Christian Temperance Union, wctu.org., n.d.

"Forever Faithful – Old Shep," RoadsideAmerica.com. 1996-2016.

"God Is On Our Side," Christianity Today, Issue 33, 1992.

"Good News, Bad News," sermoncentral.com. February, 2013.

Hedges, Chris, "What Every Person Should Know About War," New York Times, July 6, 2003.

Herodotus, "The Story of Croesus," translator, Peter Aicher, bu.edu., 2013.

"Horse Whisperer," dictionary.com., 2016.

"How Skin Grows," American Academy of Dermatology, aad.org. 2016.

Hugo, Victor, "Les Miserables," Signet Classics, New York, NY, 1987.

Knoll, Andrew, "How Did Life Begin?" NOVA, pbs.org. July 1, 2004.

Lehman, Frederick, "The Love of God," Celebration Hymnal, Word, 1997.

Markstein, Don, "The Timid Soul," toonopedia.com., 2002-03.

Miller, Calvin, The Table of Inwardness, InterVarsity Press, Downers Grove, IL, 1984.

"Origins of the Universe," National Geographic, nationalgeographic.com, 2015-2016.

Osbeck, Kenneth W., "Amazing Grace," Kregel, Grand Rapids, MI., 1990.

"Profiles in Courage: 5 Medal of Honor Recipients," military.com. n.d.

Rowling, J. K., "Harry Potter and the Sorcerer's Stone" Scholastic Press, New York, N.Y. 1998.

"Royal Styles" heraldica.org. Francis R. Velde, 2003.

Seiss, Joseph A., "The Apocalypse," Zondervan, Grand Rapids, MI., 1967.

Sproul, R. C., "What does it mean for us to call God our Father?" Ligonier Ministries, 1996.

Strong, Augustus, "Systematic Theology," Judson Press, Valley Forge, PA, 1907.

Swartz, Aimee, "Insomnia That Kills," The Atlantic, February 5, 2015.

"The Family Fallout Shelter," nebraskastudies.org, n.d.

"The Oldest Known Tablet Containing a Legal Code," informationofhistory.com., 2016.

"The Symbol of Justice," itsaboutjustice.com., 2016.

"The World's Longest Ruling Dictators," CNBC Business News and Finance. cnbc.com. 2016.

"Transcendence" store.steampowered.com, July 24, 2015.

Tozer, A. W., The Knowledge of the Holy, Back to the Bible, Lincoln, NE 1971.

Von Oech, Roger, "A Whack On the Side of the Head," Warner, New York, NY, 1983.